The Future of Foreign Aid

Other Palgrave Pivot titles

Tariq Mukhimer: **Hamas Rule in Gaza: Human Rights under Constraint**

Khen Lampert: **Meritocratic Education and Social Worthlessness**

G. Douglas Atkins: **Swift's Satires on Modernism: Battlegrounds of Reading and Writing**

David Schultz: **American Politics in the Age of Ignorance: Why Lawmakers Choose Belief over Research**

G. Douglas Atkins: **T.S. Eliot Materialized: Literal Meaning and Embodied Truth**

Martin Barker: **Live To Your Local Cinema: The Remarkable Rise of Livecasting**

Michael Bennett: **Narrating the Past through Theatre: Four Crucial Texts**

Arthur Asa Berger: **Media, Myth, and Society**

Hamid Dabashi: **Being a Muslim in the World**

David Elliott: **Fukushima: Impacts and Implications**

Milton J. Esman: **The Emerging American Garrison State**

Kelly Forrest: **Moments, Attachment and Formations of Selfhood: Dancing with Now**

Steve Fuller: **Preparing for Life in Humanity 2.0**

Ioannis N. Grigoriadis: **Instilling Religion in Greek and Turkish Nationalism: A "Sacred Synthesis"**

Jonathan Hart: **Textual Imitation: Making and Seeing in Literature**

Akira Iriye: **Global and Transnational History: The Past, Present, and Future**

Mikael Klintman: **Citizen-Consumers and Evolutionary Theory: Reducing Environmental Harm through Our Social Motivation**

Helen Jefferson Lenskyj: **Gender Politics and the Olympic Industry**

Christos Lynteris: **The Spirit of Selflessness in Maoist China: Socialist Medicine and the New Man**

Ekpen James Omonbude: **Cross-border Oil and Gas Pipelines and the Role of the Transit Country: Economics, Challenges, and Solutions**

William F. Pinar: **Curriculum Studies in the United States: Present Circumstances, Intellectual Histories**

Henry Rosemont, Jr.: **A Reader's Companion to the Confucian** *Analects*

Kazuhiko Togo *(editor)*: **Japan and Reconciliation in Post-war Asia: The Murayama Statement and Its Implications**

Joel Wainwright: **Geopiracy: Oaxaca, Militant Empiricism, and Geographical Thought**

Kath Woodward: **Sporting Times**

DOI: 10.1057/9781137298881

palgrave▶pivot

The Future of Foreign Aid: Development Cooperation and the New Geography of Global Poverty

Andy Sumner

Co-Director, King's International Development Institute, King's College London

Richard Mallett

Research Officer, Overseas Development Institute, London

© Andy Sumner and Richard Mallett 2013

All rights reserved. No reproduction, copy or transmission of this publication may be made without written permission.

No portion of this publication may be reproduced, copied or transmitted save with written permission or in accordance with the provisions of the Copyright, Designs and Patents Act 1988, or under the terms of any licence permitting limited copying issued by the Copyright Licensing Agency, Saffron House, 6–10 Kirby Street, London EC1N 8TS.

Any person who does any unauthorized act in relation to this publication may be liable to criminal prosecution and civil claims for damages.

The author has asserted her right to be identified as the author of this work in accordance with the Copyright, Designs and Patents Act 1988.

First published 2013 by
PALGRAVE MACMILLAN

Palgrave Macmillan in the UK is an imprint of Macmillan Publishers Limited, registered in England, company number 785998, of Houndmills, Basingstoke, Hampshire RG21 6XS.

Palgrave Macmillan in the US is a division of St Martin's Press LLC, 175 Fifth Avenue, New York, NY 10010.

Palgrave Macmillan is the global academic imprint of the above companies and has companies and representatives throughout the world.

Palgrave® and Macmillan® are registered trademarks in the United States, the United Kingdom, Europe and other countries.

ISBN: 978–1–137–29889–8 EPUB
ISBN: 978–1–137–29888–1 PDF
ISBN: 978–1–137–29887–4 Hardback

www.palgrave.com/pivot

DOI: 10.1057/9781137298881

Contents

List of Tables	vi
List of Figures	vii
List of Boxes	viii
Acknowledgements	ix
List of Abbreviations	x
Introduction	1
Part I Aid 1.0	8
1 What Is Aid?	9
2 What Is Aid For?	21
3 What Makes Aid Effective?	28
Part II Aid 2.0	39
4 A New Vision for Aid	40
5 What Does 'Aid 2.0' Look Like?	46
Conclusions	60
Annex	63
References	74
Index	100

List of Tables

1.1	A history of aid by defined 'needs' and aid responses	12
2.1	What is aid for? Demand and supply-led perspectives	23
4.1	Estimates of the global distribution of poverty, 2008/9, 2020 and 2030	42
4.2	Total government taxes as percentage GDP and ODA as percentage GNI in 2009 or most recent year	44
C.1	'Aid 1.0' v. 'Aid 2.0': stylised characteristics	61
A.1	What determines aid 'effectiveness'? Selected cross-country studies	63

List of Figures

1.1 Aid markets: an analytical map   11

List of Boxes

1.1 A typology of aid instruments — 15

1.2 A chronology of the evolution of aid instruments — 16

5.1 The Centre for Development's Commitment to Development Index — 51

Acknowledgements

The authors would like to thank the following people for comments and discussion on various issues raised in the book and related papers: Ravi Kanbur, Stephan Klasen, Richard Manning, Richard Jolly, Jeni Klugman, Alan Winters, Lawrence Haddad, Nancy Birdsall, Sabina Alkire, Terry McKinley, Andrew Fischer, Andrew Rogerson, Jon Lomoy, Peter Edwards, Nick Dyer, Jo Macrae, Paul Wafer, Chris Pycroft, Xavier Cirera, Charles Kenny, Ben Leo, David Steven, Amy Pollard, Simon Maxwell, and Sumana Hussain. Special thanks to Ricardo Santos, Pui Yan Wong, Henrique Conca Bussacos, and Melanie Punton for research assistance. The authors would also like to thank Christina Brian and Amanda McGrath from Palgrave Macmillan for their support throughout the publication process.

List of Abbreviations

CAP	Common Agricultural Policy
CDI	Commitment to Development Index
CGD	Center for Global Development
CSO	civil society organisation
DFID	Department for International Development (UK)
EU	European Union
FCAS	fragile and conflict-affected state
GDC	global development cooperation
GDP	gross domestic product
GPG	global public good
HCAC	high capital access country
IDA	International Development Association
IFAD	International Fund for Agricultural Development
IFI	international financial institution
IFM	innovative financing mechanism
LCAC	low capital access country
LIC	low-income country
LMIC	lower middle-income country
MCAC	medium capital access country
MDGs	Millennium Development Goals
MIC	middle-income country
mn	million
MTR	marginal tax rate
NGO	non-governmental organisation
ODA	Official Development Assistance
OECD	Organisation for Economic Co-operation and Development

OECD-DAC	OECD Development Assistance Committee
pc	per capita
PPP	purchasing power parity
PRSP	Poverty Reduction Strategy Paper
R2P	responsibility to protect
UMIC	upper middle-income country
USD	United States dollar

palgrave▸pivot

www.palgrave.com/pivot

Introduction

Abstract: *At its core, this book is about responding to change: the last few decades have seen the emergence of new aid actors, new aid modalities and, perhaps most fundamentally, a new geography of global poverty. In light of these changes, this book revisits the contested literature on aid and the uncertain evidence on aid effectiveness, and seeks to lessons and findings that might help us sketch out a practical and appropriate way of 'doing aid' in the future.*

Sumner, Andy and Mallett, Richard. *The Future of Foreign Aid: Development Cooperation and the New Geography of Global Poverty.* Basingstoke: Palgrave Macmillan, 2013. DOI: 10.1057/9781137298881

The contours of the landscape of foreign aid are rapidly shifting. What we are currently seeing, in the words of Severino and Ray (2009), is a 'triple revolution' in official development assistance (ODA): goals, players and instruments are all mushrooming and evolving. New actors have emerged, from the increasingly powerful and influential 'new' donors such as China, to numerous private foundations and philanthropists. New financing and delivery modalities have been, if not fully implemented, then widely and seriously discussed – innovative finance mechanisms such as financial transaction and airflight taxes offer numerous examples. Scepticism over the impact of foreign assistance has heralded the creation of a series of nascent aid institutions, such as cash-on-delivery and output-based aid.

This 'revolution' has taken place at a time of significance. The deadline for the Millennium Development Goals (MDGs) inches ever closer, bringing a symbolic end to what have been 15 years of largely positive progress in terms of poverty reduction and aid budgets, and an increasingly animated debate about what should happen in the years following 2015.

Yet, perhaps more fundamentally, the nature of the global poverty 'problem' has changed. Whereas in 1990 over 90 per cent of the world's extreme poor ($1.25 per day) lived in countries classified as 'low income countries' (LICs) by the World Bank, in 2008 three quarters of the world's extreme poor lived in middle-income countries (MICs) (Kanbur & Sumner, 2011; Sumner, 2010; 2012a; 2012b).

Similar patterns are evident in other aspects of human development; notably in the global distribution of malnutrition, which is also increasingly moving towards MICs (Sumner, 2010) along with the global disease burden (Glassman *et al.*, 2011) and the distribution of multi-dimensional poverty which is also MIC focused (Alkire *et al.*, 2011). Furthermore, the estimates of Moss and Leo (2011) and Sumner (2012c) based on International Monetary Fund (IMF) growth projections, suggest the number of countries classified as LICs will continue to fall. Therefore the high concentration of the global poor in MICs is likely to continue, unless one makes unrealistically optimistic assumptions about the power of growth to end poverty – unrealistic because inequality often rises during periods of fast growth (see review of literature in Sumner & Tiwari, 2009).

Indeed, growth may not be enough if the poor in MICs are disconnected from a country's growth due to spatial inequality or remoteness. The poor may also be relatively voiceless in domestic governance structures, and potentially discriminated against in public services and public spending allocations regionally. Intra-country migration may be hindered or constrained by cost and administrative regulations.[1]

The positive news is that the changing distribution of poverty suggests that the cost of ending poverty will be minimal for those countries that are currently MICs, in terms of percentage of gross domestic product (GDP) (see Sumner, 2012c): In those countries that are currently lower middle-income countries (LMICs) the average cost of ending $1.25 poverty is estimated to be in the range of 0.2%–0.6% of GDP in 2020, and by 2030 the cost of ending $2 poverty is also likely to be in a similar range. However, the estimated cost of ending $1.25 poverty in LICs is likely to remain high even in 2020 and 2030. This suggests that, for a relatively small number of countries (24–30 LICs), external support for poverty reduction will remain essential. However, the cost of ending poverty in those countries that are currently upper middle-income countries (UMICs) is already negligible.

In other words, what we are seeing is a new geography of global poverty and a new landscape of foreign aid. In this context, the very definition of what aid is and what it hopes to achieve is on the table for discussion, and the path is potentially set for the design of a new kind of development assistance and global public policy.

Much has been written on aid in the last decade or so. Dambisa Moyo's *Dead Aid*, Bill Easterly's *White Man's Burden* and Jeffrey Sachs' *End of Poverty* represent but a handful of well-known contributions to the debate. For Moyo, the problem is aid itself and how it makes governments responsive to donors rather than to their own people. For Easterly, aid has been distributed in the wrong way, and the aid community needs to have humbler objectives rather than big blueprint plans; aid should be implemented with local contexts in mind and at a grassroots level, with accountability, evaluation and reward mechanisms all built into its design. On the other hand, for Sachs what is needed is more aid and more big plans.

But these contributions are just the tip of the iceberg. There is a burgeoning, and ever growing, literature on aid effectiveness – that is, the question of whether, and under what conditions, aid might be said to 'work'. This is a literature dominated by cross-country econometric studies, which have tended to produce more disagreement than consensus. In addition, while we have seen a number of attempts to improve the way in which aid is done – from Easterly's focus on the local to Barder's

(2009a) call for greater transparency and accountability – others are stepping back from the aid paradigm altogether, questioning whether 'traditional ODA' is dead (Severino & Ray, 2009; 2010), and beginning to explore alternatives for global development cooperation. Fischer (2010), for example, asks whether contemporary aid effectiveness debates have missed the point by obsessing over the quality or quantity of aid, rather than discussing wider and more embedded structural issues.

As made clear above, the context for aid has changed quite dramatically over the last decade or so. We have seen the emergence of new actors, new modalities and, perhaps most fundamentally, a new geography of global poverty. In light of these changes, this book revisits the contested literature on aid and the uncertain evidence on aid effectiveness, and seeks to identify key findings that might help sketch out a practical and appropriate way of 'doing aid' in the future.

When one asks what aid is specifically for (or what it should be for), there are a whole range of replies – many of which are not consistent or complementary. On the 'demand side' we can identify the following: aid is for making progress on the MDGs; promoting good (enough) governance; incentivising pro-poor policy, democracy assistance and promotion; growth-led poverty reduction; trade facilitation; improving 'quality of life', rewarding political will, pro-poor or needs-based targeting, the mediation of structural imbalances within both recipient countries and the international political economy; or catalysing internal paths of development, knowledge management and transfer, technology transfer, and/or the provision of public services. Of course, poverty reduction more generally is also a popular answer, and is one which, in some ways, circumnavigates the complexity by focusing on a 'difficult to disagree with' outcome and covering for the most part all of the above.

Given these differences of opinion over the objectives of aid, it is hardly surprising that questions of whether, what kinds, and under what conditions aid might be said to 'work' remain highly contested. As Bourguignon and Sundberg (2007: 316) note:

> The empirical literature on aid effectiveness has yielded unclear and ambiguous results. This is not surprising given the heterogeneity of aid motives, the limitations of the tools of analysis, and the complex causality chain linking external aid to final outcomes. The causality chain has been largely ignored and as a consequence the relationship between aid and development has been mostly handled as a kind of 'black box'. Making further progress on aid effectiveness requires opening that box.

And Kenny (2008: 334) goes further:

> Most aid effectiveness studies tend to find little or no significant link between aid flows and economic growth in general, but many do find such a link if they split or condition results by recipient characteristics ('good policy' recipients, those with 'strong institutions' or 'non-tropical' recipients), by type of aid (netting aid for social sectors or particular donors) or by timing (post-cold war and before). As a result, it might be accepted that recent concessional loans (rather than grants) ..., for investments with short-term returns ..., to rich countries ..., currently receiving little aid ..., with strong ownership of proposed projects including co-financing ..., reasonable macro-policies ..., strong institutions ..., cool climates ..., and just coming out of a negative trade shock..., are likely to be some of the aid flows most positively associated with growth....Having said that, many of the above results appear fragile.

Compounding this great uncertainty is a rapidly changing global context for aid and development cooperation, a context that forms the backdrop to this book. Most of the world's poor already live in MICs such as India, Nigeria, Pakistan and Indonesia; a trend that is likely to both continue and deepen. This is the new geography of poverty. Looking ahead, there will be fewer and fewer 'poor' countries over the coming decades, meaning the demand for 'traditional aid' within these countries – that is, resource transfers – looks set to weaken. As a result, resource transfers will continue to go to an ever decreasing number of LICs, many of which will be affected by fragility and conflict, while for MICs something different will be required. MICs and their donors will need to agree an algorithm for reducing aid as economies grow, perhaps increasing the share of loans and/or building partnerships beyond national governments and with local government, non-governmental organisations (NGOs) and the private sector.

One take on this shift of the global poverty burden to MICs is that world poverty is becoming a problem of national rather than international distribution, and that governance and domestic taxation and redistribution policies are becoming more important than ODA. Another is that a new kind of multilateralism is needed, not only because the responsibilities to reduce poverty are shared, but also because new MICs may not want development assistance of the traditional bilateral sort.

Indeed, MICs are less and less likely to need or want resource transfers over time; instead, they will likely be more concerned with 'policy coherence' (by which we mean favourable development policies – such as a preferential trade policy). Further, it is unlikely that taxpayers in donor countries will be comfortable with resource transfers to countries that have substantial domestic resources.

At the same time, 'traditional' donors are likely to be increasingly concerned about equity and governance issues, as well as drivers of progressive change. It is true that many MICs may be able to support their own poor people to a certain extent, but inequality remains an important issue. The poor often lack a voice in governance structures, and their governments may lack political will, even when domestic resources are on the rise. In such cases, traditional donors might seek to direct their activities towards supporting inclusive policy processes and the media, social movements, civil society organisations (CSOs), and other drivers of change. Doing so may not be well received by MIC governments; many of them will be donors themselves and perhaps less interested in 'progressive (domestic) change' and more in their foreign and economic policy interests. The main area of agreement might be in the arena of 'global public goods' (GPG) to address issues such as diseases and climate change, where interest in collective action is shared. Other issues might include redefining global poverty as a global public 'bad' that requires collective action.

In short, in order to respond effectively to the changing distribution of global poverty, aid donors need to adapt quickly to changing contexts and rethink aid objectives, allocations, and instruments. This book makes a contribution to this debate in two broad areas.[2] Part I provides an in-depth discussion of the existing aid system and its key components, objectives and instruments. It also reviews the aid effectiveness literature, extracting the main findings. Annex Table A1 acts as 'companion' material to this discussion, briefly summarising the findings of 47 selected aid effectiveness studies published over the last 15 years or so.

Building on Part I, Part II seeks to develop a new vision of the aid system in light of both the shifting aid landscape and recent substantive changes to the distribution of global poverty; a vision characterised by a broad-based shift from 'traditional aid' or resource transfers to global development cooperation. Or, to put it differently, an 'Aid 2.0'.

Notes

1   The recently published *Horizon 2025* report (Kharas & Rogerson, 2012) suggests that by 2025 poverty will be focused in low-income fragile states,

and that MIC poverty is transitory. This is based on one optimistic projection that implies $2 poverty in many MICs will be largely eliminated due to economic growth in those countries. In fact, their data optimistically projects that all $2 poverty will be eradicated in India, Pakistan and Indonesia by 2015/6. However, if one generates a range of estimates using poverty data an alternative picture emerges that produces a very different prediction – that in 2020 and 2030 poverty is split between LICs and MICs fairly evenly in various growth scenarios (see Sumner, 2012c).

2   This book is first and foremost the product of a survey of key international peer review journals (in development studies and development economics) between 1990 and present, complemented by grey literature from relevant academic organisations, institutes and think-tanks. The search strategy used was as follows. A list of key search terms was first drawn up – e.g. 'aid'; 'official development assistance'; 'development cooperation' – and inputted into a number of social science databases, including Academic Search Premier, EBSCOhost, InformaWorld, IngentaConnect, Project MUSE, Sage Journals Online, ScienceDirect, Web of Science and Wiley Online Library. The individual archives of key economic and development journals were also searched in order to ensure that any articles missed by the database search were included. The websites of several major academic organisations, institutes and think-tanks were also searched for relevant grey literature. These searches produced an initial list of 304 potentially relevant articles. The next stage involved sorting the references by importance and relevance of the reference in relation to the following 'meta-question': what do the changes in global poverty distribution (towards MICs) mean for the future of aid/development cooperation? Papers were graded as either an A, B or C paper ('A' being the most relevant to the meta-question). A final list of 123 'A' references was compiled and deemed appropriate for inclusion in the review based on the fulfilment of the following two criteria: (a) published in a peer review journal or from a reputable international research institute; and (b) relevant to addressing the meta-question (see full list in references).

Part I
Aid 1.0

1
What Is Aid?

Abstract: *In this opening chapter, we argue that the aid system can be usefully viewed as a market characterised by a series of factors which determine the supply of and demand for aid. Such an approach helps us identify the multiple, overlapping (and sometimes competing) objectives of aid. The chapter also explores the wide range of aid instruments on offer and traces recent shifts and evolutions in the landscape of aid.*

Sumner, Andy and Mallett, Richard. *The Future of Foreign Aid: Development Cooperation and the New Geography of Global Poverty.* Basingstoke: Palgrave Macmillan, 2013. DOI: 10.1057/9781137298881

One way to approach the huge array of writing and research on foreign aid is to draw upon the concept of 'aid markets' (see for discussion, Barder, 2009a; Djankov et al., 2009; Dudley & Montmarquette, 1976; Easterly, 2002; Klein & Harford, 2005a). This model views the aid system as a market characterised by factors determining the demand and supply of a set of aid 'products'. It also recognises the political economy intrinsic to all markets. This should not be taken too literally, however: as Abegaz (2005: 437) notes, 'the market metaphor is not always apt, but it is still useful to recast the aid relationship as the interplay of demand (uses) and supply (sources)'.

Sketching out the aid market, Barder (2009a) argues that problems with aid are largely due to imperfect markets. More specifically, he discusses incomplete information, 'broken feedback loops', multiple and competing objectives, principal-agent problems (i.e. the interests of aid funders versus the interests of staff of aid agencies), and collective action problems. In order to improve the way aid markets function, 'market mechanisms should be complemented by international cooperation on regulatory frameworks, and investments in networked collaboration to increase access to information and draw on the wisdom of crowds' (Barder, 2009a: 3).

One could argue that the global aid market is constructed around the interaction of five stylised aspects: the demand for aid; the supply of aid; aid 'products' or instruments; aid effectiveness determinants; and trade-offs or opportunity costs (see Figure 1.1). We deal below directly with the demand for and supply of aid, and discuss aid instruments and issues around the domains of aid utility and trade-offs throughout this book.

The demand for aid is generated by some determination of recipient 'need'. This was originally conceptualised as the 'savings gap' and 'foreign exchange (forex) gap' (cf. Chenery & Strout, 1966; Chenery & Eckstein, 1970; Griffin, 1970; Papanek, 1973; Rosenstein-Rodan, 1961). However, one could add several more gaps in terms of 'need', such as a 'poverty gap' (the cost to end poverty in the country, in terms of the number of poor people multiplied by their average distance from the poverty line); a 'capacity gap' (the ability to deliver poverty reduction, perhaps proxied imperfectly by the World Bank's data on 'quality of public administration'); and a 'politics gap' (meaning the elite's commitment to poverty reduction, proxied imperfectly by the World Bank's data on 'social inclusion and equity'). Such gaps will differ to some considerable extent within LICs, MICs and fragile and conflict-affected states (FCAS).

What Is Aid? 11

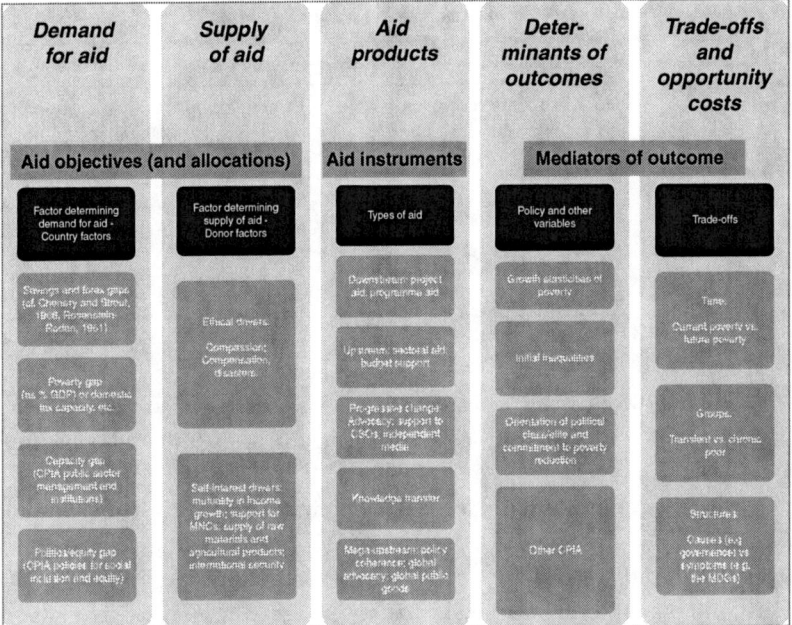

Figure 1.1 Aid markets: an analytical map
Sources: Barder, 2009a; 2009b; Burnside & Dollar, 2000; Collier & Dollar, 2001; 2002; Llavador & Roemer, 2001; Mosley *et al.*, 2004; Sayanak & Lahiri, 2009; Verschoor & Kalwij, 2006.

Of course, the demand for aid is also generated via rent seeking and other means (proxied, once again imperfectly, by the World Bank's data on 'transparency, accountability and corruption in public sector' ratings).

The supply of aid is closely related to why donors give aid. On this, Sumner and Tribe (2011) suggest there are two main reasons (which break down further): an 'ethics/compensation driver'; and 'a self-interest driver'. Again, these will differ by LIC/MIC/FCAS, but they will also differ by 'new' donors (such as India, Brazil and China) versus 'old/traditional' donors, Development Assistance Committee of the Organisation for Economic Co-operation and Development (OECD-DAC).

Further, on the question of why aid agencies exist, Barder (2009a: 8–9) identifies three key reasons relating to reducing the cost of delivering aid: i) to mediate the competing interests of donors, recipients and others; ii) to reduce transaction and information costs; and iii) to achieve returns to scale in aid management, particularly in terms of knowledge, expertise and systems. Of course, the supply for aid is also generated via geopolitical interests and the personal views of ministers.

TABLE 1.1 A history of aid by defined 'needs' and aid responses

	Demand for aid – defined 'need'	Supply of aid – aid instruments
1950s–70s	Capital shortage (domestic and forex); knowledge and technology shortage	Project and program aid (BoP) and technical assistance
1980s–90s	Stabilisation and structural change, debt	Structural Adjustment Loan (SAL), sector SAL and HIPC
Mid 1990s–	Capacity, recurrent financing, institutions	Budget support (general and sectoral)

Source: Developed from Kanbur (2003: 5).

Such an approach resonates with Kanbur's (2003: 5) discussion of the history of aid and the shifting demand for, and supply of, aid over time (see Table 1.1).

Normative definitions of foreign aid remain relatively conventional despite a changing world (Severino & Ray, 2009). As Radelet (2006: 4) explains, the standard definition of aid generally comes from the OECD-DAC: 'financial flows, technical assistance, and commodities that are (1) designed to promote economic development and welfare as their main objective... and (2) are provided as either grants or subsidised loans'. Grants and subsidised loans (where there is a 'grant element' of at least 25%) are categorised as concessional financing, whereas loans that carry market terms are considered non-concessional financing.

Official Development Assistance (ODA) is the most widely recognised form of aid. In 2010, the total ODA contributed by DAC countries was 129 billion USD, or roughly 0.32% of DAC Gross National Income (still way off the UN-endorsed 0.7% target). In addition, it has been estimated by Kharas (2007: 7) that, outside the DAC, at least 29 other countries are giving 'significant amounts' of aid annually, including Brazil, Russia, India, China (the BRICs), Saudi Arabia and the UAE. Tentative calculations put this non-DAC contribution at around 10% of global bilateral aid (ECOSOC, 2008), a substantial – and increasingly important – composition of international aid flows which has started to attract considerable attention (see Manning, 2006; Mawdsley, 2010; 2012; Paulo & Reisen, 2010; Wood, 2008).

In order to qualify for ODA, countries have to be classified as potential recipients by the OECD-DAC. The list is reviewed every three years (Fink & Redaelli, 2010: 14). Clearly, some countries receive more ODA than others, although this is dependent on how ODA flows are measured – for example, while Bangladesh received 1.4 billion USD of aid in 2004, this was equivalent to just 2% of GDP or roughly 10 USD per person. In contrast, São Tomé and Principe received 33 million USD in the same year, but this worked out as 67% of GDP or about 209 USD per person (Radelet, 2006: 5).

According to Radelet (2006: 6), ODA tends to be 'one of the largest components of foreign capital flows to low-income countries, but not to most middle-income countries, where private capital flows are more important'. However, as he also points out, declines in aid do not necessarily correspond with increases in private capital; aggregate data can obscure the fact that increased private capital flows may be concentrated in just a small number of MICs.

ODA can target and promote specific 'transmission channels' or 'mechanisms' for growth, such as investment, imports, public sector fiscal aggregates, and government policy (Gomanee et al., 2005a). However, ODA is also used to finance, amongst other things, direct budget support (Vidal & Pillay, 2004), Sector-Wide Approaches (SWAps) (Foster, 2000), climate change mitigation efforts (Michaelowa & Michaelowa, 2005), and social protection programming (Giovannetti, 2010) such as state-run programs designed to provide non-contributory cash payments to the poor (Künnemann & Leonhard, 2008).

Moreover, different countries supply different types of aid. For example, while Indian assistance tends to consist primarily of non-monetary aid (mainly in the form of technical assistance and scholarships), China tends to offer a wider mix of monetary and non-monetary aid, the former of which is usually tied to the use of Chinese goods and services (McCormick, 2008). The OECD-DAC is reasonably clear about what counts as ODA and what does not. Any money spent on military aid, peacekeeping and counter-terrorism, for example, is not reportable as ODA.

According to Fink and Redaelli (2010: 2), humanitarian assistance 'is meant to provide rapid assistance and distress relief to populations temporarily needing support after natural disasters, technological catastrophes, or conflicts', and is considered a separate type of aid in accordance with its foundations in humanitarian law. Similarly, Demekas et al. (2002) argue that post-conflict aid should be split into humanitarian aid and reconstruction aid, and that analyses of aid effectiveness should deal with each separately. In practice, however, the distinction between humanitarian aid and ODA is not always clear-cut. There are rarely clear delineations marking when or where relief ends and development begins; indeed, relief and development have come to be viewed as occupying a continuum rather than distinct categories (Sollis, 1994). This makes it difficult to identify the moment when humanitarian assistance starts feeding into and shaping longer-term developmental objectives.

Definitional debates aside, ODA has been increasingly directed towards FCAS over recent years, blurring distinctions in the process. In 2008, for example, 33.2 billion USD, or 30% of global ODA flows, was channelled to FCAS (OECD, 2010). Much of this is spent with developmental objectives in mind, such as achieving progress towards the MDGs, but there has also been an increase in financing 'ODA-related security activities' (Oxfam, 2011). The propensity of some bilateral donors to design their aid allocation and spending patterns in accordance with national security interests (i.e. addressing the problems of FCAS in order to shore up the 'global borderlands') also calls into question the objectives of ODA. Additionally, there are certain caveats within the OECD definition of ODA which give rise to a further blurring of what counts as the 'economic development and welfare of developing countries'. For example, temporary assistance to refugees from developing countries arriving in donor countries is reportable as ODA during the first 12 months of stay, as are all costs associated with repatriation (OECD, 2008).

So, there are a great many types, instruments and products of aid (see Box 1.1 for a typology and Box 1.2 for an approximate chronology of instruments below). The multiplicity of aid products matters within the context of different country classifications. For many, the fact that increasing numbers of MICs have become aid donors is a compelling argument that they should no longer qualify as aid recipients. Rostoski (2006) considers the aid relationship between Germany and China, concluding: 'the central government in Beijing has...accumulated the necessary financial means to solve the problems [associated with poverty] in its own country without foreign assistance' (Rostoski, 2006: 543). He insists that Germany should stop giving financial aid and concentrate instead on providing technical assistance and advice. Further, in an assessment of German aid to Namibia (an upper MIC), Amavilah (1998) stops short of calling for an end to aid, but finds that German direct foreign investment and trade seem more preferable than aid. Although German aid to Namibia is 'clearly important' to the country's economic growth, even the short-term impacts are found to be small. Yet, others argue that MICs still require aid, and indeed that aid can play an important role in their continued development. For example, Jaradat (2008: 271) points out that many MICs face 'considerable challenges' which necessitate the continuation of aid.

BOX 1.1 A typology of aid instruments

According to Ohno and Niiya (2004: 5), over the last 50 years, aid modalities have evolved in response to emerging development priorities (e.g. from capital shortages to structural reforms to government capacity building). Subsequently, today there are multiple 'types' of aid. A number of authors have argued for the disaggregation of aid into its various types in order to refine conceptual models and policy analysis (e.g. Mavrotas, 2005; Ouattara, 2007; Suhrke & Buckmaster, 2006). In light of the numerous instruments listed below, this certainly makes a great deal of sense. It is, of course, important to note that in practice there may be some overlap between the different types of aid (Severino & Ray, 2009: 21).

Broadly speaking, **financial aid** can be either **concessional** or non-concessional. Concessional aid refers to **grants** or **subsidised loans** (where there is a 'grant element' of at least 25%), while non-concessional aid refers to **loans** that carry market, or near market terms. Aid can also be **tied**, although this practice is becoming less popular. **Official Development Assistance** (ODA) is the most well-known form of financial aid. ODA is bound by OECD-DAC rules.

Disaggregating financial aid further, there is **project aid** and **program aid**.

Project aid can: use government systems (i.e. the donor-supported project can still be part of the government budget); use parallel systems (i.e. where the donor has taken the lead in design and appraisal); or go through NGOs/private providers.

Over the years the role of project aid has diminished and the role of program aid has increased, evolving into **Sector Wide Approaches** (SWAps). SWAps are government-led and require that all significant public funding for the sector supports a particular sector policy and expenditure program thus harmonizing approaches across the sector. Under this arrangement, aid often comes in the form of **pooling funds**. **Sectoral budget support** can be **earmarked** meaning that aid must be spent on specific expenditure categories within the sector.

There has also been a shift from **structural adjustment operations**, such as **balance of payments support** and **Structural Adjustment Programs** (SAPs), to **general budget support** which aims to institutionalize a new kind of aid relationship between donors and recipients. This involves new conditionality contracts which are ex-post, policy-linked, empirically based, country-specific, and more country-driven. **Poverty Reduction Strategy Papers** (PRSPs) are an example of this approach, and aim to build better donor-recipient partnerships and integrate civil society more effectively into the policy process (see also the Paris Declaration principles).

Financial aid can operate at different scales or levels. It can be **upstream** (i.e. policy and institutions) or **downstream** (i.e. implementation). Aid can also be used to fund **debt relief**, to increase the financial resources available to the recipient government.

Non-financial aid includes **food aid** and **technical assistance**.

Humanitarian assistance can be split broadly into **relief aid** and **reconstruction** aid, although this distinction is often blurred in practice. Leader and Colenso (2005) list a number of instruments available to donors working in FCAS: **program aid (BoP support, debt relief, budget support); technical cooperation/assistance; project aid; social funds; joint programs** and **pooled funding; multi-donor trust funds; global funds** and **partnerships;** and **humanitarian assistance**.

BOX 1.2 *A chronology of the evolution of aid instruments*

An aid instrument typology can also be drawn chronologically as follows (dates have been left deliberately open-ended to indicate that many of the instruments are still in use):

'Traditional' (1950s–)
- **Project and programme** aid aimed at financial transfer
  - Typically balance-of-payments support
  - Prevalence of 'stand-alone' projects

- **Technical assistance** projects
  - Project, program and technical aid all consistent with **knowledge transfer**

'New' (1990s–)
- Move away from single projects to project 'clustering': **pooling funds** under the **Sector Wide Approach** arrangement
  - Initially called the **Sector Investment Program**
- Focus on structural issues
  - Rise and fall of **Structural Adjustment Programmes**

- Rise of 'new conditionality': ex-post, country-specific; Paris Declaration
  - **PRSPs**
  - **Civil society capacity building**
  - **Social protection**
  - Includes instruments such as **cash transfer programs**. Involves building up state capacity

'Innovative' (Present–)
- Innovative financing/**Innovative Financing Mechanisms** (IFMs)
  - Market-based approaches to development finance; public-private partnerships; engaging new networks and groups (e.g. consumers, private companies, foundations) in finance models
  - A 'mushrooming' of actors and channels
- **Global Public Goods/Regional Public Goods**
- **Policy Coherence**
  - Not new *per se*, but of increasing importance. Can be thought of as an alternative to direct or formal resource transfer

Sources: Demekas et al., 2002; Foster & Leavy, 2001; Leader & Colenso, 2005; Ohno & Niiya, 2004; Radelet, 2006; Severino & Ray, 2009.

Severino and Ray (2009) have argued that our conventional understanding of ODA is looking more and more outdated; increasingly irrelevant as a tool for action. International development assistance is today tasked with three conceptually distinct subsets of objectives: first, accelerating the economic convergence of developing and industrialised countries; second, providing or basic human welfare (guided predominantly by the MDGs); and third, finding solutions for the provision and preservation of global public goods (Severino & Ray, 2009: 5). Since the 1990s, there has been an end to the state's monopoly over development assistance. Not only have the size and number of major international NGOs expanded, but we have also begun to witness the emergence of a range of new actors, from private foundations (e.g. the Gates Foundation) and businesses (e.g. Project (RED)), to transnational thematic funds (e.g. GAVI). Additionally, there is now an array of different sources of funding and aid channels. For example, at the 2010 MDGs Summit, the

Leading Group on Innovative Financing for Development proposed a 'Global Solidarity Levy' which would be used to finance global public goods (Giovannetti, 2010: 50).

Innovative financing mechanisms (IFMs) and climate financing are two particular areas receiving increasing interest both in policy and academic arenas (see, for example, de Ferranti, 2006; Jones, 2010; Ketkar & Ratha, 2009; Lob-Levyt & Affolder, 2006; McCoy, 2009). Such initiatives represent a marked departure from existing and past means of development financing (e.g. ODA) and 'traditional' donor-recipient arrangements, and, in many cases, have been successful at engaging new stakeholders and different kinds of donor networks. IFMs are incredibly diverse, ranging from airline and tobacco taxes and advance market/purchase commitments to global public-private partnerships and health funds. Many adopt explicitly market-based approaches, and many attempt to integrate consumers and the private sector more directly in the development financing process. However, while expectations of IFMs are high (Jones, 2010), robust assessments and evaluations are somewhat limited to date.

Many of the new actors and sources of aid can be grouped into Develtere and De Bruyn's (2009) 'fourth pillar' of development cooperation, defined as: 'organisations, institutions, and private initiatives... [which] draw on their experiences in their own communities and economies in the North... [and] forge ties with their counterparts and communities in the South' (Develtere & De Bruyn, 2009: 913). These include trade unions, farmers' associations, social movements, schools, hospitals, foundations, migrant organisations, companies and sports clubs – ostensibly 'non-specialist' organisations. It could be argued, however, that this classification is slightly too restrictive, and that we could also include within this 'fourth pillar' South-South development cooperation initiatives (i.e. non-governmental relationships). For example, the Hewlett Foundation has recently begun to fund Southern-based think-tanks which will no doubt share output and knowledge with donors, NGOs, community-based organisations, CSOs, and other think-tanks around the world. This is an important area to consider within the realm of aid instruments, as such initiatives may give rise to new and alternative forms of knowledge which may well diverge considerably from mainstream views on development. Additionally, new funding channels are opening up. As Develtere and De Bruyn (2009: 917) point out, taking unregistered remittances into account, the total volume of money sent back home by migrants each year exceeds twice or more the global ODA budget.

Further, some recent discussions have explored the possibility of 'policy coherence as aid' (e.g. Katseli *et al.*, 2006; Ratha *et al.*, 2011; Xenogiani, 2006) such as and the Center for Global Development (CGD)'s 'Commitment to Development Index' (see later discussion and CGD, 2012). Such an approach entails 'donor' countries adopting certain policies on issues that are favourable to 'recipient' countries, such as migration, trade, and climate change. At a minimum, these policies could be built upon a 'do no harm' approach (e.g. in relation to trade rules). Policy coherence aims to optimise policy choices for the mutual benefit of countries in both the North and South, and goes 'beyond aid' to tackle the structural constraints which keep many poor countries poor. More open migration regimes, for example, would likely have a significant impact on poverty reduction in developing countries through remittances, employment generation, and human capital accumulation (Anyanwu & Erhijakpor, 2010).

While it is still common to think of aid in terms of traditional ODA flows, there are numerous and increasing sources and instruments of aid that traditional understandings of ODA fail to capture. As Severino and Ray (2009) argue, ODA no longer represents an adequate benchmark for a world increasingly gearing towards global public policy rather than development assistance: ODA measures the wrong things, and only provides us with a (roughshod) measurement of the means to achieve 'progress' without ever really defining what results and outputs should be aimed for.

It is worth bearing in mind that this evolving landscape has both positive and negative implications. Although funds may be enlarged and more options and strategies made available, what we are presented with is an increasingly complex, crowded, and potentially fragmented aid landscape (Knack & Rahman, 2004; Severino & Ray, 2010). Desai and Kharas (2008: 166) suggest that private aid has the ability to sit 'above political influence', comparing it favourably with traditional ODA flows. However, while private channels and innovative models certainly hold the potential to:

> reduce political interference... the evidence suggests that development priorities [in such models] are often set in a top-down manner, thereby giving a weak voice to beneficiaries, and insufficient support has been given to capacity building of key domestic actors (e.g. the recipient country public sector). (Jones, 2010: 12)

In sum, while aid has traditionally been viewed as a resource transfer of grants or concessional lending (e.g. OECD, 2010: 2), the range of available aid instruments is constantly expanding and diversifying. We have seen the emergence of both new 'upstream' aid products and instruments (e.g. policy coherence in trade, climate, migration/remittances; advocacy for and support to independent media and CSOs; and global public goods), and new 'downstream' aid products and instruments (e.g. project aid or program aid for service delivery), as well as completely new financing mechanisms that include private and public contributions. Cutting to the chase, then, what all of this suggests is that 'aid' may no longer be the right word to describe what might be more accurately termed 'international cooperation'.

2
What Is Aid for?

Abstract: *Aid is assigned multiple objectives. Whilst not always complementary or mutually reinforcing, many of these objectives revolve around the core task of promoting poverty reduction (usually via economic growth) in the Global South. This chapter reflects on the findings of a range of academic studies into the drivers of allocation decisions and, in so doing, highlights the complex, multi-layered nature of aid systems.*

Sumner, Andy and Mallett, Richard. *The Future of Foreign Aid: Development Cooperation and the New Geography of Global Poverty.* Basingstoke: Palgrave Macmillan, 2013. DOI: 10.1057/9781137298881.

When we ask what aid is for, on the 'demand side' we can identify the following: the MDGs (Baulch, 2006); good (enough) governance (Grindle, 2004; 2007); incentivising pro-poor policy (Sayanak & Lahiri, 2009); democracy assistance and promotion (Santiso, 2001); growth-led poverty reduction (Barder, 2009b); trade facilitation (Hoekman & Nicita, 2010); improving 'quality of life' and social development (Kosack, 2003); rewarding political will (Hermes & Lensink, 2001); pro-poor, needs-based targeting (White, 2001); the mediation of structural imbalances both in domestic countries and the international political economy (Fischer, 2009); catalysing internal paths of development (Pronk, 2001); knowledge management and transfer (Samoff & Stromquist, 2001); technology transfer (Benarroch & Gaisford, 2004); and the provision of public services (Pessoa, 2008). An alternative view to the question of what aid is for might be emancipation from aid as an objective in itself – meaning aid to end aid by building other sources of revenue or 'catalytic aid' (Rogerson, 2011).

In terms of what aid is for on the 'supply side', we can identify: political and strategic interests (Alesina & Dollar, 2000; Riddell, 2007); the domestic political situation of the donor and the type of government in office (Fleck & Kilby, 2006); commercial interests (Macdonald & Hoddinott, 2004; Ostrom et al., 2001); donor commitments to democratic governance and human rights (Berthelemy & Tichit, 2002; Gillies, 1999; Neumayer, 2003); global security imperatives (Patrick & Brown, 2006; Sachs, 2005a); moral imperatives and compassion (Riddell, 1986); and compensation (for colonialism, slavery and climate change, policy incoherence, etc.) (see Table 2.1).

It should be noted that demand and supply side factors are not always or necessarily neatly divisible in this way.

More than 20 years ago, McGillivray (1989) assessed the extent to which donors base their aid allocations on the relative needs of recipient countries. Using an income-weighted per capita aid index and data for 85 recipient countries between 1969 and 1984, he found marked differences in donor performance. While Belgium, Finland, Denmark and Norway scored higher than all other DAC member states, countries such as the United States performed poorly. Further, the combined per capita allocations of multilateral agencies were found to outperform those of DAC bilateral donors, suggesting that the latter tend to be more influenced by political, strategic and commercial – i.e. 'non-developmental' – interests in their allocation decisions.

TABLE 2.1 *What is aid for? Demand and supply-led perspectives*

	What is aid for?	Aid is required to address or promote...	Example references in recent literature
Demand side	Savings gap and forex gap	Structural imbalances; trade facilitation	Fischer, 2009; Hansen & Tarp, 2000; Hoekman & Nicita, 2010
	Poverty gap	Pro-poor economic growth; social development	Barder, 2009b; Kosack, 2003
	Capacity gap	Knowledge transfer; technology transfer; public service provision	Benarroch & Gaisford, 2004; Pessoa, 2008; Samoff & Stromquist, 2001
	Political gap	Democratic processes; good governance; incentivise political will for poverty reduction	Grindle, 2004; 2007; Hermes & Lensink, 2001; Santiso, 2001
Supply side	Compassion	To reduce human suffering	Berthelemy, 2006a; Younas, 2008
	Compensation	As compensation for colonialism; unfair trade and investment patterns; climate change	Brown & Stewart, 2006; Edgren, 2002
	Mutuality in income growth/welfare	Improve welfare of both donor and recipient	Sayanak & Lahiri, 2009
	Supply of raw materials, agricultural products and other capital goods	To support commercial interests of donors	Baulch, 2006; Berthelemy, 2006a; Younas, 2008
	International security	Ensure 'spillovers' from conflict and fragility don't create international problems; to support geopolitical interests of donors	Berthelemy, 2006a; Hattori, 2001; Patrick & Brown, 2006; Riddell, 2007; Sachs, 2005a

Source: Authors development of discussion in Sumner & Tribe (2011).

McGillivray's study highlights two key points. First, that the performance and selectivity of donors is heterogeneous. Second, that how we define 'performance' is important. McGillivray's index was based on per capita income, and he states in his conclusion that, for the purpose of the study, 'one donor can be said to outperform another if it allocates a greater proportion of its aid to poor and highly populated countries' (McGillivray, 1989: 566).

The aid allocation model developed by Collier and Dollar (2001; 2002) has proven particularly influential in donors' allocation strategies. The Collier-Dollar model of 'poverty efficient' aid allocation aims to maximise the number of people pulled out of poverty by favouring countries with 'good' policies. This model is based on simple logic – give more aid to countries where there is more poverty and where aid will have more impact on poverty – and it claims to maximise the impact of aid on global poverty reduction. Although the concept of 'poverty efficient' aid allocations is difficult to disagree with, there is much divergence in opinions over certain aspects of the approach. For example, Anderson and Waddington (2007: 5) have pointed out that in reality efficiency is determined by effectiveness, which is in turn affected by numerous, widely contested factors, and that countries with higher levels of poverty may miss out if their environments are not considered conducive to efficient poverty reduction.

In reality, decisions behind aid allocations and selectivity are far more diverse and complicated. According to Baulch (2006: 933–4), there are many reasons why donors give aid to developing countries, including: colonial and commercial ties; concerns about governance; institutions and absorptive capacity; the attitudes of recipient governments towards donors; and geopolitical considerations (see also Riddell, 2007). Clearly, not all of these relate to 'poverty efficiency'. Some appear to be more about the self-interest of donors than poverty reduction in recipient countries and, indeed, ODA can sometimes be explicitly designed to benefit the donor. For example, many bilateral donors have historically 'tied' portions of their ODA – although the practice is becoming less widespread – meaning that recipients are required to use the aid to purchase goods and services from firms in the donor country.

Frequently cited in discussions on aid spending is a study by Alesina and Dollar (2000) which finds that donor allocations are driven as much by political and strategic considerations as by recipients' economic needs and policy performance. They argue that allocation patterns – commonly inconsistent with the 'demand side' of aid markets – are partially responsible for why aid has not had more of an impact on growth and poverty reduction. They find that each of the 'big three' donors allocate large chunks of their aid to strategic allies (the United States), former colonies (France), or in ways highly correlated with UN voting patterns (Japan). They also report a clear trend for 'democratisers' to receive a substantial increase in aid.

Further, as Wood (2008) points out, despite its influence, in practice aid allocations have diverged widely from the Collier-Dollar model, with more aid allocated to Africa than some have recommended. Wood (2008) also brings to the fore the important issue of time in aid allocations. He argues that while the Collier-Dollar model is myopic, concerned only with current and short-term gains, most donors are forward-looking and interested in addressing future poverty. He proposes retaining the central core of the Collier-Dollar model – allocating aid in a 'poverty efficient' way – but adopting future poverty reduction as a key objective, meaning that the revised model would regularly adjust for the decline of future poverty.

Many other studies have investigated models and drivers of aid allocations. Anderson and Waddington (2007) discuss 'country-by-country target allocation', a recently proposed alternative to the 'poverty efficient' model that does not penalise countries for low aid effectiveness, but which likely results in smaller reductions in poverty at the global level. Weiss (2008) on the other hand argues that a new donor consensus has emerged in recent years, built around the central themes of economic growth, good governance and social development; these are perceived to be interlinked and mutually reinforcing (the reality, of course, is not quite as straightforward). Meanwhile, Berthelemy (2006a) finds that aid allocation behaviours result from a combination of self-interest and altruistic purposes. This mixture of (often competing) aid motives and objectives helps account for why donors are not necessarily responsive to changes in recipient countries' institutional and policy conditions when 'efficient' aid allocation models dictate that they should be (Nunnenkamp & Thiele, 2006).

Until now, many have tended to view aid allocations to MICs as inconsistent with a genuine desire for global poverty reduction. In other words, aid to MICs has generally been seen as a kind of aid market 'failure'. For example: as noted above, the index constructed by McGillivray (1989) classifies donors who allocate to countries with higher per capita incomes (i.e. MICs) as poor performers; Koch *et al.* (2009) similarly construct the 'neediest' countries as having low per capita incomes; Wood (2008) suggests that 'motives other than poverty reduction' might explain why MICs receive far more aid than the Collier-Dollar model of 'poverty efficiency' recommends; and Baulch (2006) notes that the 'regressivity' of the United States' and the EC's spending patterns (both are found to spend the majority of their aid budgets in MICs) is inconsistent with efforts to achieve the MDGs. Further, while some studies have reported an MIC 'bias' in donor allocations – for example, Levin and Dollar (2005) find that between 1992 and 2002 MICs received more ODA than both LICs and 'difficult partnership countries' (an earlier label for fragile states) – many others have not. Indeed, there is also some evidence that, because it is more likely to depend on the geostrategic and political concerns of donors than on poverty reduction goals, aid to MICs tends to be more volatile than flows to other countries (Levin & Dollar, 2005: 22).

There are thus many possible objectives of aid. These may be seen as overlapping, competing or complementary, but certainly complex and likely co-evolving, therefore leading to greater uncertainty about whatever outcome might emerge. Yet, studies into aid effectiveness tend to frame the impact of aid in terms of its ability to generate economic growth (Feeny & McGillivray, 2010: 899). As Radelet (2006: 7) states, 'economic growth has always been the main yardstick used to judge aid effectiveness', and there is also some credence to White's (2001: 1062) argument that studies which emphasise the role of growth in poverty reduction (e.g. Collier & Dollar, 2002) have been particularly influential in shaping donors' allocation and spending strategies.

Following this, we can plausibly postulate that one primary (normative) function of foreign aid is to augment economic growth in developing countries. In keeping with this general outlook, an increasing number of commentators have added a further layer of complexity, developing this 'aim' by placing a greater importance on the need for 'pro- poor growth'; that is, economic growth that at least reduces poverty (Verschoor & Kalwij, 2006). However, not only is the ability of growth to generate poverty reduction heterogeneous across countries (and largely a product of a whole range of factors – most notably initial inequality – see for review Sumner & Tiwari, 2009), but the actual ability of aid to create growth is wildly contested, and some studies have found that aid in fact tends to increase consumption rather than sustained growth (Arellano *et al.*, 2005).

Moreover, this represents a relatively narrow framing of aid. While it is true that many see economic growth, or pro-poor economic growth, as the overriding purpose of foreign aid, there are a number of alternative views within the literature as to what aid is, could be or should be used for. For example, and as noted above, it is generally accepted that the political and commercial interests of donors play an important role in defining aid allocations (Baulch, 2006; Berthelemy, 2006a; Riddell, 2007; Younas, 2008). In a way, the fulfilment of such interests can thus be understood as a desired outcome of aid. Meanwhile, more critical observers point to the system's cultural and symbolic power politics, as 'recipients become complicit in the existing order that enables donors to give in the first place' (Hattori, 2001: 633); in this sense, aid is seen to play an instrumental role in attempts to preserve the dominant organisation of global hierarchies of power (see also Hayter, 1971; Hayter & Watson, 1985).

While 'poverty reduction' is often used as a short-hand for promoting widespread, poverty-reducing economic growth, in reality there are a series of trade-offs and sacrifices which come at the expense of facilitating such growth (see Barder, 2009b; also Figure 1). By focusing solely on the growth aspect of poverty reduction, donors risk marginalising other legitimate objectives, such as reducing chronic poverty or providing social services. In contrast, by adopting too many diverse objectives, donors risk negatively affecting the performance of aid (Edgren, 2002), adding numerous, co-evolving layers of complexity and resulting in greater uncertainty.

There is, therefore, a strong case to be made for reducing our expectations of aid. In LICs, for example, one might argue that, 'aid agencies should set more modest objectives' (Easterly, 2003: 39–40), and there is today wide agreement that aid is no panacea. The juxtaposition of different sets of recipient 'needs' and donor objectives, combined with the challenges of heterogeneous contexts, translates into processes that are highly complex and outcomes that are highly unpredictable.

3
What Makes Aid Effective?

Abstract: *This chapter focuses on the mediating factors that determine the outcomes of aid. The last twenty years or so have seen the publication of a bewildering array of academic studies into aid effectiveness, yet there remains considerable debate as to whether, and under what conditions, aid can be effective. The chapter reviews the findings of a range of selected studies (which are also summarised in Table A1 in the Annex) and closes with a number of conclusions to inform a new vision for aid.*

Sumner, Andy and Mallett, Richard. *The Future of Foreign Aid: Development Cooperation and the New Geography of Global Poverty*. Basingstoke: Palgrave Macmillan, 2013. DOI: 10.1057/9781137298881

What Makes Aid Effective? 29

In this chapter we drill down into the expansive literature on aid effectiveness in an attempt to make some sense of the ocean of econometric evidence on the subject. Table A1, located in the Annex, summarises the findings of 47 selected aid effectiveness studies and can be treated as companion material to this chapter.

The interaction of demand and supply in aid markets generates aid objectives, allocations and products (aid instruments), and leads to a variety of outcomes depending on a whole range of mediators. These mediators, or mediating factors, ultimately shape the effectiveness of aid, and are thought to include: levels of corruption and the composition of public expenditure (Mosley et al., 2004); the extent of social expenditures (Verschoor & Kalwij, 2006); the growth elasticity of poverty (Heltberg, 2002); social capital and institutions (Baliamoune-Lutz & Mavrotas, 2009); the commitment to poverty reduction and orientation of the political class/elite (Angeles & Neanidis, 2009; Webster & Engberg-Pedersen, 2002); plus the kinds of domestic policies adopted, notably macroeconomic policy (Burnside & Dollar, 2000; Collier & Dollar, 2002 – although this finding has been strongly critiqued by Dalgaard et al., 2004; Easterly et al., 2003; Hansen & Tarp, 2000).

When thinking about outcomes, it is also important to consider potential trade-offs or opportunity costs, such as: pursuing short run versus long run poverty reduction; lifting the 'cheaper' poor (i.e. the transient poor, those near the poverty line) versus the more 'expensive' poor (i.e. the chronic poor, those whose poverty is characterised by longevity, and/or severity and/or a multiplicity of deprivations) out of poverty; focusing on the headcount poverty versus the poverty gap (see Kanbur & Sumner, 2011); and tackling the causes of poverty versus the symptoms of poverty (Barder, 2009b). Additionally, there are also important technical, macroeconomic aspects of how aid is actually used that play a large role in what outcomes will be observed (see Killick & Foster, 2011).

While the last twenty or so years have seen the publication of a bewildering array of studies into aid effectiveness, there remains considerable debate as to whether, and under what conditions, aid can be effective in achieving its (primarily economic) objectives.

Mavrotas (2005) suggests it is difficult to understand the impact of aid without first recognising its heterogeneity. He suggests disaggregating aid into four main types: project aid, program aid, technical assistance and food aid. Each type of aid is clearly designed with different goals in mind and is likely to operate within different institutional and political contexts. Through a case study of aid to Uganda, Mavrotas shows that different types of aid have different impacts. He finds that whereas project and food aid reduce public investment and government consumption, program aid and technical assistance have the opposite effects. Furthermore, all types of aid, with the exception of project aid, lead to reductions in government borrowing. Interestingly, and in contrast to the popular argument that aid displaces domestic revenues, Mavrotas also finds that the Ugandan government did not reduce taxation efforts under any aid type. This is consistent with the work of Clist and Morrissey (2009) who, using data for 82 countries between 1970 and 2005, find no robust evidence for a negative effect of aid on the GDP/tax ratio (on the contrary, they find that grants tend to increase tax revenue over the medium term). There is thus a case to be made for decomposing aid flows in order to avoid what Mavrotas (2005: 1021) terms 'aggregation bias' (see also Clemens et al., 2004).

Aid effectiveness as we currently understand it has been prominent since the beginning of the 1990s (Forster & Stokke, 1999). The idea of aid effectiveness, and much of the debate surrounding it, is embedded within a broader developmental paradigm, or framework, that can be described thus:

> [D]onors commit themselves to providing specific support for a national poverty reduction strategy in the form of financial and technical resources to boost national capacity, while the recipient government commits itself to improving economic and political governance in order to implement the strategy. (Hayman, 2009: 582)

This framework incorporates a number of elements institutionalised within the Paris Declaration on Aid Effectiveness, signed in 2005, such as donor harmonisation, greater domestic stakeholder participation, partnership, joint ownership, and increased accountability and transparency (see Wood et al., 2008).

Newer policies, such as Poverty Reduction Strategy Papers (PRSPs) and Multi-Donor Budgetary Support packages, go some way towards successfully operationalising the Paris Declaration's core elements (Booth, 2003; Quartey, 2005). However, as Hayman (2009) illustrates, the warm fuzziness of high-level conference discourse often belies a messier, more complex reality. There are, for example, problematic issues of trust (or lack thereof) underlying ownership arrangements between donors and recipients (Whitfield & Fraser, 2009), and multiple, competing agendas risk undermining effective collaboration between donors and recipient governments (Hayman, 2009: 595).

In terms of the empirical evidence on aid effectiveness – or, more specifically, on the question of whether and under what conditions foreign aid stimulates economic growth and reduces poverty – numerous studies are available, many if not most of which are grounded in econometric methodologies (see Annex Table A1). Statistical investigations into the impact of aid have been ongoing for several decades now, becoming particularly prominent from the early 1990s onwards.

On the face of it there seems to be little agreement on findings, both general and specific, within the econometric literature. To take but a few examples, while Loxley and Sackey (2008) report a positive and statistically significant effect of aid on growth, finding that aid increases investment (a major transmission channel in the aid-growth relationship), Rajan and Subramanian (2005) argue there is little robust evidence of a positive (or indeed negative) relationship between aid inflows and economic growth. Similarly, while Burnside and Dollar (2000) argue that aid most effectively promotes growth in a 'good' policy environment, Ram (2004) finds little empirical evidence to support the view that redirecting aid towards countries with 'good' policies leads to more growth and greater poverty reduction.

Major reviews and surveys of the aid effectiveness literature reflect these divergences, generally concluding that there are a number of key, competing findings emerging from the body of studies. A selection of some of the most recent surveys is discussed here.

According to Feeny and McGillivray (2010: 899–900), there are four main findings from the aid effectiveness literature. First, foreign aid is generally effective at spurring economic growth in recipient countries (see McGillivray *et al.*, 2006). Second, foreign aid works better in some countries or environments than in others, although the precise factors that determine the outcome of aid remain the subject of much debate. For example, while many point to the importance of 'good' economic policies in recipient countries (Burnside & Dollar, 2000; 2004; Collier & Dollar, 2002), others variously highlight the role of social policies (Verschoor & Kalwij, 2006), a democratic political environment (Islam, 2003; Kosack, 2003; Svensson, 1999), and geographic location (Dalgaard *et al.*, 2004). Third, the specific type of aid is likely to be important for its impact on economic growth and poverty reduction (Clemens *et al.*, 2004; Mavrotas, 2005; Ram, 2004). Fourth, aid has diminishing returns: Feeny and McGillivray (2008) estimate that the level of aid at which its impact on growth diminishes is, on average, roughly 20% of recipient GDP, and absorptive capacity constraints have been observed both in stable and conflict-affected countries (Clemens *et al.* 2004; Collier & Hoeffler, 2004; Dalgaard & Hansen, 2001; Hadjimichael *et al.*, 1995). This finding supports the argument that developmental problems in both LICs and MICs are not purely about a lack of resources. At the same time, however, it is worth mentioning that some studies have found evidence of negative partial growth effects of aid at low levels of aid (e.g. Gyimah-Brempong *et al.*, 2010).

On the other hand, Anderson and Waddington (2007: 4) conclude that three different sets of results have been found in the literature regarding the relationship between aid and growth. First, that aid increases economic growth in all countries, but only up to a certain point (e.g. Hansen & Tarp, 2001; Lensink & White, 2001). Second, that aid increases economic growth, but only in countries with 'good' economic policies and also only up to a certain point (e.g. Burnside & Dollar, 2000). And third, that aid has no effect on economic growth (e.g. Easterly, 2003).

In a summary of their three meta-analyses of the aid effectiveness literature (specifically, studies investigating the impact of aid on savings, investment and growth), Doucouliagos and Paldam (2009) find no evidence of a significantly positive effect of aid, and suggest that exchange rate movements (i.e. 'Dutch disease') might account for aid ineffectiveness.

Howes (2011: 5–6) argues that although 'there are a wide range of often conflicting views on aid effectiveness', these can be distinguished along two dimensions – good and bad (i.e. 'what kind of outcome?') and large and small (i.e. 'what scale of outcome?') – giving rise to 'four distinct views' as follows:

First, good and large: Aid could have a transformative effect if applied in the right way and in sufficiently large volumes (e.g. Sachs, 2005b). Second, bad and large: Aid can have a large impact, but in a negative rather than positive way (e.g. Bauer and Yamey, 1982). Third, good and small: Aid has little effect on development, but it can be a positive contributor 'at the margin' (e.g. Birdsall *et al.*, 2005). Fourth, bad and small: Aid is a minor and negative determinant of development (e.g. Easterly, 2006).

These represent four contrasting perspectives, and there are various studies which lend support to each. But how can such a degree of divergence arise in the first place? Howes (2011: 8) argues, there are a number of reasons why assessing aid effectiveness is so challenging: it is difficult to establish the counterfactual; evaluations are difficult when certain high-level indicators are used, the determinants of which are poorly understood; the heterogeneity of recipients makes it difficult to draw broad conclusions; and the fact that there are many types of aid, each with different objectives, each affected by different factors.

Empirics aside, there is also a lack of consensus on the nature of the relationship between foreign aid and economic growth from a theoretical perspective (Hermes & Lensink, 2001: 3), and the complex and multiple linkages that connect the spending or allocation of aid with outcomes are characterised by high degrees of uncertainty. Abegaz (2005: 439) argues that when one goes beyond cross-country regressions, 'it becomes clear that the effectiveness of development aid is also thwarted by a long and poorly understood economic transmission mechanism that links aid and growth'. He considers (the uncertainty of) four links in particular:

- Between aid and policy reform: Evidence suggests that aid cannot buy reform in countries where the government expresses little desire for it (e.g. Svensson, 2000). Indeed, in the absence of 'growth-promoting institutions', large aid inflows may even be counterproductive insofar as they disincentivise the mobilisation of domestic resources;
- Between aid-related reform and 'productive' investment: Evidence suggests that most aid tends to increase government consumption (e.g. Boone, 1996; Devarajan et al., 2004);
- Between investment and growth: Aid boosts demand in the short term (with possible adverse effects via real exchange rate appreciation), and enhances supply in the medium- to long-term through expanding capacity.
- Between growth and poverty reduction: Aid tends to benefit the non-poor and the urban population disproportionately. The inability of governments to provide universal access to basic services prevents the poor from taking full advantage of opportunities provided by aid-related activity (See Bourguignon & da Silva, 2001; Hansen & Tarp, 2000).

There is also some contention regarding the validity of some econometric studies. For example, much of the (influential) econometric research into aid effectiveness has been criticised by Roodman (2007) for failing to include robustness testing. He argues that fragile results are the norm rather than the exception within the cross-country aid-growth literature, and that econometric studies are yet to teach us much about whether and when aid works. Agenor *et al.* (2008) agree; reinforcing Dollar and Easterly's (1999) argument that the links between aid and growth are not robust, they claim that 'reduced-form regressions of the aid-growth link are largely inconclusive' and that average estimates formed through cross-country regressions can be meaningless (Agenor *et al.*, 2008: 279). In addition, Doucouliagos and Paldam (2009: 456) report that aid effectiveness studies tend to suffer from a highly significant 'reluctance bias': 'If an AEL [aid effectiveness literature] researcher finds several results he/she will be reluctant to report those that suggest that aid causes harm'.

Making clear sense of the extensive aid effectiveness literature is a highly challenging exercise. Nonetheless, and taking the aforementioned criticisms into account, there are still some broad points upon which most (or at least many) would probably agree.

First, the idea that aid can play a role – whether in terms of promoting economic growth (e.g. Collier & Dollar, 2001) or aggregate welfare (e.g. Gomanee *et al.*, 2005b), or whatever other outcome is desired – but that there are many factors beyond 'good' recipient policies that mediate its impact (McGillivray, 2003: 2). Such factors within recipient countries might include, inter alia: the colonial experience (Angeles & Neanidis, 2009); the level of environmental vulnerability (Guillaumont & Chauvet, 2001); and whether they are experiencing negative terms of trade shocks (Collier & Dehn, 2001).

The idea that aid can potentially make a difference is consistent with McGillivray *et al.*'s (2006) argument that practically all research published since Assessing Aid (World Bank, 1998) agrees that aid works to the extent that in its absence (i.e. in a counterfactual scenario), growth would be lower. Elsewhere, McGillivray (2006: 17) argues that 'the sheer weight of evidence emerging from the literature is such that one can clearly reject the hypothesis that aid, on aggregate, has no beneficial impact on or is harmful for growth'.

Similarly, in a literature review, Morrissey (2001) concludes that the general picture is one of aid contributing positively to growth (and investment). To sum up, while the impact of aid is always heavily circumscribed, mediated as it is by a multiplicity of factors, very few people are calling for its termination.

Second, domestic institutions and politics are mediating factors. The main idea here is that aid can play a role but that its impact is dependent to a substantial degree upon internally-driven processes largely outside the control of external actors. For example, through a review of literature, Dollar and Easterly (1999) find that domestic institutional and political features determine policy reform (which may in turn improve aid effectiveness), but that external assistance is unlikely to generate reform in a country in which there is no domestic drive for it.

Although donors use aid to encourage recipient governments to enact market reform and develop privatisation policies, research by Banerjee and Rondinelli (2003) finds that foreign aid has no systematic impact on the privatisation process. Privatisation, as with institutional change, is predominantly a domestic process.

The key difference between this point and the first is that while many mediating factors are unalterable – such as those mentioned above (e.g. colonial experiences, geographical location) – domestic institutional and political landscapes are not immutable. Thus, given the historical and continuing resistance of internal processes to external manipulation, aid effectiveness is, to some degree at least, outside the control of donors. Subsequently, it might pay to be more cautious in our expectations of aid (Easterly, 2003; Kenny, 2008).

Third, the influence of the 'supply side' of the aid market on allocations and spending likely impedes aid effectiveness (from the perspective of the 'demand side'). As Alesina and Dollar (2000: 55) argue, aid allocations based on self-interest may be very good at promoting strategic interests, but the trade-off is that it 'has only a weak association with poverty, democracy, and good policy'. Linked in to this is also the generally accepted view that bilateral aid allocations tend to be more affected by strategic, political or commercial interests than are multilateral aid allocations. The influence of the 'supply side' is also detrimental to aid effectiveness in a different sense: the increasing number of donors, of funding sources, and of aid instruments means that aid flows risk a number of consequences (e.g. funding overlaps, competing donor objectives, and fragmentation).

One might also tentatively pose as a fourth point that disaggregation is (becoming increasingly) important. Aid effectiveness studies investigate multiple dimensions of the impact of aid; they look at how it affects private investment, public investment, domestic expenditure, government consumption, public savings and more, many of which are considered transmission channels for growth (see Gomanee et al., 2005a). Delivering a verdict of aid based exclusively on studies which focus on just one or two of these dimensions does not equate to robust analysis. Likewise, the specific types of aid flows matter, as do the political and institutional features of individual recipient countries (see point 2). Not all LICs or MICs have the same requirements, and some will react differently to different types of aid. The need to break down categories (of aid flows and country classifications) is also becoming increasingly important given the recent emergence of new donors, innovative financing sources/mechanisms, and alternative aid instruments (Severino & Ray, 2009; 2010). Navigating this complex and crowded landscape requires more disaggregated analysis.

Kenny (2008) provides a good example of disaggregated aid effectiveness analysis, arguing that, taking into account the importance of institutions to aid outcomes as well as the fungibility of aid flows, 'programmatic aid should be expanded in countries with strong institutions, while project aid should be supported based on its ability to transfer knowledge, test new practices and/or support global public good provision' (Kenny, 2008: 330–1).

Disaggregation also calls for differentiating between different types of countries. Many have already done this. For example, within the broader aid effectiveness literature, there is a body of studies focusing on aid to FCAS. A number of econometric studies have found evidence showing positive impacts of aid in the post-conflict period: Collier and Hoeffler (2004) report that aid is most effective when introduced between three and seven years after the 'end' of war due to a doubling of absorptive capacity; Demekas *et al.* (2002) find that post-conflict reconstruction aid tends to raise the equilibrium level of stock and does not necessarily lead to a contraction of the tradeable goods sector; and Elbadawi *et al.* (2007) find a non-significant or negative long-term correlation between aid and real exchange rates, suggesting there is little prima-facie evidence for Dutch disease. On the question of absorptive capacity, studies have also found that aid inflows to post-conflict countries are constrained by saturation points: for example, Collier and Hoeffler (2004: 7) estimate the saturation point during post-conflict periods. In addition, the finding that the initial post-conflict years are not responsive to aid seems to suggest that conventional donor policy built around 'substantial surges of aid flows' needs rethinking (Elbadawi *et al.*, 2007).

There is, however, considerable disagreement over the impact of post-conflict aid. For example, Suhrke *et al.* (2005) 'retest' Collier and

Hoeffler's original study using stricter measures of what constitutes civil war, and find that aid has up to less than half the proposed effect on growth between years three and seven – supposedly key years of the post-conflict phase. Indeed, they argue, any growth stimulated by extra aid injections would be negligible (0.26%). Additionally, Suhrke and Buckmaster (2006: 337–8) argue that Collier and Hoeffler's research is based on highly aggregated data and a small number of observations. Their approach is to disaggregate the data and look at comparative case studies. They report a number of findings: high levels of post-war aid and rapid economic growth are not necessary preconditions for sustained post-war peace; aid levels and economic growth rates are not clearly related to the quality of peace; aid can help stabilise peace in the short term, and is compatible with sustained peace in the longer term; and political contexts of donation and implementation have considerable influence on aid patterns.

Some studies suggest that aid flows to MICs may suffer from particular problems of their own. Levin and Dollar (2005: 22–23), for example, argue that aid to MICs is likely to be more variable than aid to LICs for two reasons. First, geostrategic and political interests – which are more prone to change from year to year – are likely to trump poverty reduction objectives in donors' decisions to allocate to MICs. And second, MICs are at a higher risk of balance-of-payments shocks, meaning donors are likely to be exposed to more risk in these countries than in LICs.

In terms of ways forward, it is worth continuing to clarify and question some of the core assumptions that underpin mainstream approaches to aid effectiveness. As Kenny (2008: 340) points out, there has been too little work investigating the role of aid in achieving goals other than income growth. Similarly, White (2001) casts reservations over the idea perpetuated by some econometric approaches and studies that growth is the only channel through which aid is able to reduce poverty, and points out that the hugely influential Collier-Dollar results have been strongly criticised by a number of studies, including Hansen and Tarp (2000) and Lensink and White (1999). White also questions what exactly is meant by 'good policy', particularly in relation to facilitating pro-poor growth as opposed to 'just good old fashioned growth' (White, 2001: 1062). On this, Hermes and Lensink (2001) argue that the set of particular reform policies which should be adopted depends on a country's 'level of development'. Thus, if LIC and MIC classifications are sufficiently robust indicators of levels of development, then there are implications for what should constitute a 'good policy' environment in each. According to Hermes and Lensink (2001: 15):

> In a low-developed country the political and economic institutional framework will not be as developed, which means that liberalisation efforts should be considered very carefully.

Similarly, in a review of the key developments in the literature on aid, institutions and governance since the 1990s, Booth (2011: 22) asserts that the 'right' institutions are always context- and time-period-specific, and that part of the reason why institutions are so important is because they ultimately frame likely policy choices. There are clearly assumptions here about the relationship between levels of development (based on GNI per capita) and institutional frameworks. But if these can be made explicit, then it might be possible, following Hermes and Lensink, to demarcate good policies in accordance with LIC and MIC categorisations. Clarifying what a good policy environment looks like in different countries would then lay the foundation for improving aid effectiveness. This supports point four of the aid survey – the importance of disaggregation.

Given that there are a number of factors which mediate the effect of aid in developing countries, we now know that, in most cases, improving aid effectiveness is not a simple case of increasing resources. Indeed, at the very least, sudden large increases 'could not fail to have large balance-of-payments, monetary and fiscal consequences, posing real challenges for macroeconomic management' (Killick & Foster, 2011: 84). Yet, as Booth (2011: 23) points out, the limited success external actors have had so far in shaping institutional change should not be a reason for disengagement, not a reason to revert to conditionality. Instead, he argues, the experience thus far calls for more politically informed, more context-sensitive and less supply-driven aid. Such a call is consistent with recent efforts to shift the emphasis of aid analyses towards country-specific frameworks which aim to better understand internal political and institutional processes.

Part II
Aid 2.0

4
A New Vision for Aid

Abstract: *The starting point for this chapter is that the nature of the global poverty 'problem' has changed and continues to evolve. We discuss future poverty projections and growth scenarios, and outline the implications of a new geography of global poverty for donors and international development more broadly.*

Sumner, Andy and Mallett, Richard. *The Future of Foreign Aid: Development Cooperation and the New Geography of Global Poverty.* Basingstoke: Palgrave Macmillan, 2013. DOI: 10.1057/9781137298881

A New Vision for Aid   41

The focus of Part I of this book was the aid system as it currently is – in particular, the objectives, instruments and impact of aid. This lays the groundwork for Part II. In light of the shifting landscape of foreign aid, the changing distribution of global poverty, and the current level of understanding of what aid can and cannot achieve, Part II seeks to sketch out a new vision for aid in the future.

A point of departure is to consider how the future might look using different growth scenarios. This can be done by drawing upon an approach taken in Karver *et al.* (2012) and Sumner (2012c) which involves generating three different growth scenarios as follows:

- An optimistic scenario assumes that for 2009–2020 and 2009–2030 average incomes will rise at the average annual growth rate of the GDP Purchasing Power Parity (PPP) per capita (pc) data in the IMF's World Economic Outlook (WEO 2012) for the period 2009–2016 (2011–2016 data are projections).
- A moderate growth scenario assumes that from 2009 average incomes will grow at an average annual growth rate of the GDP PPP pc for the period 2009–2016, minus 1 per cent on the basis that this is the average error historically observed in IMF growth estimates/projections (as per empirical analysis of Aldenhoff, 2007).
- A pessimistic growth scenario assumes that from 2009 average incomes will grow at *half* of the average annual growth rate of the GDP PPP pc for the period 2009–2016.

These growth scenarios then generate, for each country, GDP PPP and Gross National Income (GNI) pc forecasts for 2020 and 2030. The former, GDP PPP pc can be used to estimate poverty in 2020 and 2030 (although the assumption of static inequality must be made), and the latter, GNI pc, can be used to estimate country classifications in 2020 and 2030.

By taking the poverty and distribution survey data from PovcalNet (World Bank, 2012), and the 2020 and 2030 population estimates from the UN (medium variant), we can estimate the number of poor people in 2020 and 2030 in each country, as well as the poverty gap as a proportion of GDP (PPP USD, constant 2005 international USD).

Two essential caveats must be noted: First, such projections are *an inherently imprecise exercise* that merely illustrates possible future scenarios (See also discussion in Kanbur & Sumner, 2011; Karver *et al.*, 2012;

Kenny & Williams, 2001). Second, the approach likely overstates poverty reduction in fast growing economies such as LMICs, because it assumes static inequality in countries that are rapidly growing.

Even so, the data suggests that the remaining poverty in those countries that are currently MICs will remain at least half of all world poverty in 2020 and 2030 (see Table 4.1). And given that some countries that are currently LICs will move into the MIC category, there could be just one third of world poverty in LICs in 2020 and 2030. As GDP rises, the cost of ending poverty as a proportion of domestic GDP will (likely) fall, and poverty will become increasingly about national distribution, with the potential exception of some countries, many of which are in sub-Saharan Africa.

The projections for 2020 and 2030 show that the number of LICs in 2020 could be in the range of 24–30, and in 2030 from 16–28, compared to the current 35. Using the moderate growth scenario, in 2020 poverty will be largely split as follows: 60 per cent in countries that were MICs in 2010, and 40 per cent in countries which were LICs. In 2030, global poverty will be split more evenly between countries that are currently LICs and countries that are currently MICs (see Table 4.1). This suggests that even if inequality does not rise, poverty will remain an issue for MICs – and, as noted, a number of the countries that are currently LICs will be MICs by then too.

However, one should remember the caveats noted above – that this endeavour of making projections for income/expenditure poverty is *an inherently imprecise exercise* that merely illustrates possible future scenarios. In terms of other dimensions of poverty such as education,

TABLE 4.1   *Estimates of the global distribution of poverty, 2008/9, 2020 and 2030 (moderate growth scenario; e = estimate)*

	Global distribution of $2 poverty (% world poverty)		
	2008/9	2020e	2030e
Low-income countries (current group)	20.6	39.7	46.5
Lower middle-income countries (current group)	59.2	54.6	47.5
Upper middle-income countries (current group)	20.2	5.7	6.0
Estimated remaining LICs in 2020/2030	–	33.8	35.7

Source: Data from Sumner (2012c).

Notes: Estimates derived by using method of Karver *et al.* (2012) and processed from PovcalNet (World Bank, 2012) and WEO (IMF, 2012), based on static inequality. Note: For method see text.

nutrition and health in particular, historical trends can be used to produce approximations for 2030 with a greater level of credibility (see Karver et al., 2012).

What do such patterns mean for development cooperation? If one accepts that the objective of ODA is poverty reduction, as Barder (2009b: 3–4) argues in his discussion of aid agencies' mandates, then a means of assessing poverty reduction 'need', either now or in 2020 or 2030, would be the cost of ending poverty (the poverty gap in USD) for each country as a percentage of GDP or some other variable (see Kanbur & Mukherjee, 2007 for a relevant discussion of the quantification of the 'relative ability' to eradicate poverty).

A new aid allocation model might, therefore, be usefully based on a formula that accounts for 'needs to end poverty' either now or in 2020 or 2030, as well as 'potentially available domestic and global resources'. 'Needs to end poverty' could first be assessed by multiplying the number of poor people by their average distance from the poverty line. This would provide an indication of the total resources needed to 'end poverty', which could also be worked out as a percentage of GDP. A country's capacity to 'end poverty' would thus depend, in part, on levels of 'potentially available domestic and global resources', which can be estimated using proxies such as foreign exchange reserves, access to capital markets, and capacity for domestic taxation.

One idea would be 'aid to end aid'; or, in other words, 'catalytic aid' (see Rogerson, 2011). Arguably, the ultimate sign a country is no longer poor is that it no longer has a need for foreign assistance in the form of aid flows (or perhaps that a country becomes a foreign aid donor itself, although that would make India and China non-poor countries). At present, the concept of 'catalytic aid' appears vaguely defined, but, broadly speaking, it would be about reducing aid as a percentage of GDP or total government spending or total investment. In practice, over the course of a number of years, a country's development strategy would aim to progressively reduce its aid-to-GDP ratio by setting intermediate targets for aid as a proportion of total investment, and/or aid as a proportion of total government revenue. Alternatively, one could opt for switching gradually from grant aid to concessional loans, and then finally to non-concessional loans. Indeed, many MICs may already be at or close to this point.

All of the above would require redirecting considerable amounts of foreign aid away from 'traditional' programs (e.g. schools, bednets, vaccines) and towards things like building domestic tax systems, addressing capital flight, and hiring corporate lawyers in order to get better deals for countries when negotiating natural resource contracts with international companies. Over a long run, this would imply a huge shift in the tax burden from the middle classes in the North towards the new middle classes and elites in the South, which of course might not be politically well received in the South, at least not initially. Further down the line, however, such a shift might result in increased government responsiveness to the interests and demands of those funding the state – their own taxpayers.

Recent empirical evidence for this is provided by Devarajan et al. (2011: 15), who identify that there is a positive relationship between the level of tax revenue and the extent of voice and accountability in a country. Table 4.2 shows that, as average income rises, total taxes as a proportion of GDP rises too. And at the same time as average income rises, aid is becoming less and less significant as a proportion of GNI in new MICs. There is thus a shift from external funding in the form of aid towards non-aid and domestic sources from taxation. However, if the scope for domestic taxes is constrained by many of the population being barely above the poverty line, access to aid may still be important in middle-income countries, for the near future at least.

What does all this mean for OECD donors? In order to meet their own objectives of reducing global poverty, traditional donors will need to continue work in the new MICs, where most of the poor live. Kanbur and Sumner (2011) outline four reasons to continue aid to new MICs on a case-by-case basis. First, pockets of poverty call for aid, regardless of where they occur. Second, spillover effects of MIC growth, such as climate change, may negatively affect LICs and the poor. This provides an argument for directing development assistance towards public goods and aid flows to countries that are part of the solution to the underlying negative externalities. Third, by engaging with MICs, aid agencies gain

TABLE 4.2 *Total government taxes as percentage GDP and ODA as percentage GNI in 2009 or most recent year*

	LICs	LMICs	UMICs	OECD HICs
Total government taxes as % GDP	13.0	17.7	20.7	35.4
ODA as % GNI	12.6	1.0	0.1	0.0

Source: Data from Sumner (2012c) drawing upon IMF (2011: 53–4) and World Bank (2011).

knowledge that can then be useful for development assistance to LICs, such as implementing social safety nets. Fourth, given that MICs are still part of a global political economy that may disadvantage them to some extent (e.g. in relation to trade and finance patterns), at least until those global relationships change, it could be argued there is a moral obligation to continue to provide development assistance. All of the preceding discussion suggests that a rethink of the relevance of specific aid instruments is necessary. This is particularly the case in relation to MICs, many of whom will neither need nor want ODA in future but donors can engage in MICs in new ways.

In sum, until now poverty has been viewed predominantly as an LIC issue, but if in the future there are drastically fewer poor countries then donors will need to rethink their approaches and strategies. Their partnerships and aid relationships are likely to look very different in different types of countries in terms of aid objectives, allocations and instruments. Moving forwards, in MICs, aid or international cooperation needs to address four core areas: pockets of poverty; spillover effects of MICs' growth; knowledge transfer; and mutually supportive policy coherence. These areas form the focus of the next chapter.

5
What Does 'Aid 2.0' Look Like?

Abstract: *This chapter proposes what a fresh terms of engagement between donors and middle-income countries might look like, outlining in particular four key aspects of this new relationship. First, engagement to support policy coherence across areas such as migration and trade. Second, engagement to support inclusive policy processes in middle-income countries and to reduce marginalisation by working with civil society in middle-income countries. Third, engagement to support the production and co-financing of global public goods. And fourth, engagement to support research and knowledge transfer across different country contexts.*

Sumner, Andy and Mallett, Richard. *The Future of Foreign Aid: Development Cooperation and the New Geography of Global Poverty.* Basingstoke: Palgrave Macmillan, 2013. DOI: 10.1057/9781137298881

If there are drastically fewer poor countries, what does this mean for aid instruments? In this chapter we sketch out what some of the new instruments might look like and explain how they are appropriate to the changing context.

It is likely that aid to low-income countries will still be about ODA resource transfers but also, even more so, about fragility, conflict, and post-conflict interventions. Various aid instruments have been used in LICs to date. For example, large quantities of aid have been channelled to LICs in the form of budgetary support, on the premise that this improves the effectiveness of public services. There is some evidence for this, but the findings are generally mixed. In their review of the literature, Moss *et al.* (2006: 18) conclude – tentatively, it is important to add – that a 'large and sustained volume of aid can have negative effects on the development of public good institutions in low-income countries'. It is also argued that aid disincentivises domestic revenue collection (Heller & Gupta, 2004: 412) and undermines the social contract between citizen and state (Moss *et al.*, 2006), thus impeding the development of effective formal (public) institutions. Further, foreign aid inflows inadvertently permit governments to channel their own expenditure into other sectors or projects, effectively allowing them to sidestep their obligations towards public service provision and poverty reduction – this is otherwise known as aid fungibility. However, not all research supports this negative outlook. Ouattara (2006), for example, examines the impact of aid flows on public sector behaviour in developing countries, finding that aid does not discourage revenue collection efforts. Additionally, Moore (2004) explains that the (multilayered) relationship between aid and state formation is far from clear, and that multiple outcomes have been observed. Finally, McGillivray and Morrissey (2000) argue that fungibility itself is not a particularly important concern.

Other instruments include 'aid for trade' or trade facilitation schemes – for example, Hoekman and Nicita (2010) consider the significance of market access terms to poor countries, and argue that the pursuit of trade facilitation is particularly important for LICs; as such, donors should provide resources to LICs in order to improve trade facilitation. Yet there are problems with these too. For example, there are several issues surrounding the opening up of markets and trade regimes in both LICs with nascent industries and weak institutions (see for example Chang, 2002), as well as in fragile states (Baliamoune-Lutz, 2008).

Donor approaches to aiding LICs have thus far tended to focus on growth, and there is little reason to suspect that this will change dramatically over the coming years. Social protection programs, particularly cash transfer interventions, are also on the rise, propelled by promising – yet not problem-free – experiences in Latin America and sub-Saharan Africa (see Devereux, 2006; Holmes et al., 2010; Rawlings, 2004). Such programs have also recently been linked to MDGs and human rights agendas (Künnemann & Leonhard, 2008).

Donors can also use aid to support and promote human rights and civil liberties. Fowler (2000b), following van Tuijl (2000), argues that in countries without adequate resources (that is, typically LICs), NGOs can help people to act as claimants of basic entitlements. This entails framing poverty in human rights terms, and framing development in explicitly more political terms. This option might also include democracy promotion and assistance (see Santiso, 2001).

Increasingly, if the remaining LICs are FCAS, aid to LICs will likely be framed by institution and state-building imperatives. Recent years have seen the adoption of state-building as a frame for engagement in fragile states (OECD, 2007; World Bank, 2011). Indeed, both normatively and in practice, peace-building has come to be understood, in effect, as state-building, with donors viewing a strong and legitimate state as obligatory for securing a stable (although not necessarily just) peace, and for catalysing economic development. Indeed, there is a good body of support for such an approach within the academic literature (for example, Cammack et al., 2006; Cramer & Goodhand, 2002; Paris, 2004; Roberts, 2008), and a strong, viable and legitimate state may indeed be necessary for the roll-out of effective social programs (Harvey et al., 2007). Thus, building viable states is likely to be central to ensuring that the basic needs and welfare of those countries' citizens are met. That said, the limits to aiding FCAS have been identified by Feeny and McGillivray (2009), who point out that donors have justifiable concerns about the effectiveness of aid to fragile countries. They carry out an absorptive capacity analysis and find that a number of FCAS receive far more aid than they can efficiently absorb (from a purely per capita growth perspective). They go on to argue that absorptive capacity is an important, and context-specific, issue, and that it warrants further attention whilst recognising the diversity of fragile and conflict-affected states.

While some of the above aid instruments may be valid for MICs, in general development assistance to MICs will likely evolve considerably because ODA/resource transfer will be needed less and less as domestic resources expand. However, concessional loans will still be useful even if grants are not appropriate. One reaction will be for donors to simply disengage from MICs. An alternative is a new kind of multilateralism.

Drawing on Kanbur and Sumner (2011), it is possible to construct an approach to donors-MICs engagement on the following rationale:

i. The continuing dominant position of OECD countries in global trade and investment (although this is changing) and unfavourable development policies suggests donors' most important engagement with MICs (and all countries) lies in policy coherence.
ii. In MICs there are surprisingly large 'pockets of poverty' in otherwise prosperous countries due to marginalisation and donors can support inclusive policy processes by supporting MIC civil society organisations (CSOs) to improve prospects for more inclusive development.
iii. There are MIC growth spillovers in neighbouring countries, and LICs and aid can seek to address these spillovers via co-financed global public goods.
iv. MICs hold considerable banks of knowledge on poverty and development; the transfer/sharing of which with LICs (and vice-versa) could be supported via aid.

We discuss each of these elements in greater detail below. It is important to note that in MICs, given their diversity, future development assistance will need to be tailored appropriately further. For example, emerging powers such as India and Indonesia, for instance, have little need for ODA as a resource transfer, but still have substantial poor populations. Large MICs affected by fragility and conflict, such as Nigeria and Pakistan, also have large numbers of poor people and may have limited need for ODA, but state capacity for poverty reduction may be a significant constraint. Meanwhile, stagnant but stable MICs may need ODA resource transfers in order to catalyse economic growth and support productive capacities, and there are also a number of fast growing LICs that will likely graduate to MIC status in the near future – Ghana is one recent example of such a transition. In the following discussion we focus on four aspects that cut across all donor-MIC engagement.

i. Donor-MIC engagement to support development policy coherence

Policy coherence is about developed or industrialised countries making their own national policies more consistent with their stated objectives to promote growth and reduce poverty around the world (Kapstein, 2005: 120). For example, Berthelemy et al. (2009) find that for countries with a per capita income of less than US$7,300 (PPP 2000 prices), a tightening of migration policy is equivalent to a reduction of the level of aid by about 24 per cent. Therefore, they conclude that a trade-off exists between aid and migration policies.

According to Picciotto (2005: 314), examples of potential policy incoherence, whereby developing countries are negatively affected by the policies of rich countries, include: EU farming subsidies and the Common Agricultural Policy (CAP); EU fishing subsidies; tariffs on industrial goods, such as steel and textiles, imposed by OECD countries; patents and the protection of intellectual property rights; a lack of controls regarding CO_2 emissions; and the international promotion of counter-terrorism measures in poor countries that lack budgetary resources for even basic social programs.

In addition, a policy coherence analytical framework can also be used to highlight the contradictions of existing aid instruments. For example, there is little point in promoting aid for trade or trade facilitation schemes if the international structural constraints are such that aid recipient countries are disadvantaged by unfair market access terms.

'Policy coherence' in the development-related policies of traditional donors is not new – it has been discussed for some considerable time (see, for example, Forster & Stokke, 1999). For example, the OECD Development Centre's Policy Coherence project aims to investigate the interaction of rich-country policies in poor countries, including their interdependence with local policies (Mayer, 2006: 5); and since 2003 the Center for Global Development (CGD) in Washington has published the Commitment to Development Index (CDI). The CDI scores the performance of developed countries in seven key areas – aid, trade, investment, migration, environment, security, and technology – awarding points for policies and actions which support poor countries' developmental efforts, broadly defined (see Box 5.1). Scores are also adjusted in accordance with the size and characteristics of the rich country in question.

There is new potential for a much greater demand from new MICs for greater policy coherence.

BOX 5.1 *The Centre for Development's Commitment to Development Index*

- *Aid* – Quantity, net of debt payments; tying; selectivity; project proliferation; tax breaks for charity.
- *Trade* – Tariffs; quotas; farm subsidies; actual imports.
- *Investment* – Political risk insurance; environment and labour screens; fighting international bribery; double taxation; other measures related to foreign direct investment (FDI) and portfolio investment.
- *Migration* – Immigration, especially unskilled; foreign students from developing countries; aid to refugees and asylum-seekers.
- *Environment* – Greenhouse gas emissions; gas taxes; fishing subsidies; tropical timber imports and other measures.
- *Security* – Spending on personnel to UN peacekeeping; personnel to non-UN; arms exports; protecting sea lanes.
- *Technology* – Public R&D spending; tax breaks for R&D; limiting intellectual property rights.

Source: CGD (2012).

ii. Donor-MIC engagement to support inclusive policy process and reduce marginalisation in otherwise prosperous countries by working with MIC civil society to improve prospects for more inclusive development

As Eyben *et al.* (2004: 24–5) point out, tensions within aid relationships appear to be particularly striking in middle-income countries: 'many of the larger MICs have more complex and diverse institutions both within and outside government and donors can find themselves involved in internal political conflicts through the choice of whom they decide to associate with'.

Within most if not all countries, there are various actors and organisations pushing for progressive change (however defined). We can note, for example, civil society organisations, women's organisations, social movements, workers' unions, rights-based organisations, and independent media as all playing important roles in the mission to promote progressive agendas. But what role can donors play in supporting these elements of civil society? There is little point in pretending that this does not cross over into the political domain – indeed, one could argue that this constitutes an explicitly political approach infused with liberal values. For example, Hearn (1999) finds that CSOs committed to the promotion of liberal democracy and economic liberalism are the most popular with donors. Yet, donors also link into global citizenship movements, underpinned by universal human rights.

On this 'traditional' approach to supporting change agents – meaning CSOs – there is a considerable body of literature on civil society in developing countries to draw upon (see, for example, Frantz, 1987; Hadenius & Uggla, 1996; Howell & Pearce, 2000; Robinson, 1995) as well as the 'drivers of change' approach and numerous case studies (see for discussion DFID, 2005; Moore, 2001; Warrener, 2004).

And, of course, efforts to support Southern-based CSOs are not new. For example, Howell and Pearce (2000: 75) remarked more than a decade ago that there was considerable funding for projects to strengthen CSOs in developing countries. In addition, increasing the visibility of civil society in policymaking processes has been a core element of PRSPs (Molenaers & Renard, 2002).

Howell (2000: 7) outlines three broad approaches that donors have adopted in order to support and develop civil society: institution and capacity building, partnerships and coalitions, and financial sustainability. In practice, she explains, these approaches are not clear-cut and tend to overlap. The third donor approach outlined above by Howell – (ensuring) financial sustainability – highlights the importance of CSOs' and other organisations' material bases. The performance and impact of many, if not most, CSOs tend to be constrained by insufficient resources (e.g. money, time). And as Howell (2000: 8) points out, the opportunities for Southern-based NGOs and CSOs to fundraise domestically are limited due to their countries' poverty levels, small middle classes, and low levels of economic development.

There are, of course, numerous potential problems associated with externally funded CSOs. For example, to what degree will external assistance influence or manipulate an organisation's political agenda? Do CSOs risk having their views and actions delegitimised by accepting foreign assistance? Robinson and Friedman (2007) investigate how far external donor funding influences the policy engagement and outcomes of a selection of CSOs in Uganda and South Africa. Regarding the South African CSOs, they find that the source of funding, whether internally generated or externally supplied, does not seem to be a significant factor in explaining their differential policy impact (Robinson & Friedman, 2007: 659). Further, they find that one CSO in particular receives 90 per cent of its funding from foreign sources, but manages to maintain a high degree of independence in framing agendas whilst significantly contributing to public policy (Robinson & Friedman 2007: 660). Meanwhile, in Uganda they report a more mixed set of results. For example, one organisation has experienced internal ideological and factional divisions and had its viability and independence undermined by its reliance on foreign aid. Additionally, it is argued that one CSO's limited contribution to national policy debate cannot be explained by its dependence on donor funds (Robinson & Friedman, 2007: 661). In conclusion, they claim that:

> Foreign aid is not the most critical determination of successful policy engagement; the character of a particular organisation and its specific relationship to the state are decisive. But resources do matter, since the least effective organisations in terms of policy engagement... are also the least well-endowed financially. (Robinson & Friedman, 2007: 663)

In terms of funding CSOs, Robinson and Friedman (2007: 665) suggest four measures donors can take to strengthen the organisational capacity of CSOs: replace short-term project support with long-term program grants and technical assistance; provide specialised assistance aimed at strengthening capacity for policy analysis and advocacy; encourage the adoption of strategies designed to identify and institutionalise local sources of funding; and encourage governments to remove restrictive controls and simplify NGO registration procedures, thus promoting a more supportive policy environment for CSOs. Their third proposed measure is consistent with Aldaba *et al.*'s (2000: 678) argument that one of the ways NGOs can become self-sustainable in a 'beyond aid scenario' is by taking better advantage of domestic resource options.

Donors can also engage in 'partnership work' in middle-income countries. Eyben *et al.* (2004: 14) describe how a very small financial investment in strengthening the relationships between a country's state government, its civil society, and an international financial institution (IFI) can bring about significant shifts in social policy. Larbi-Jones (2004), for example, points to the work of the UK's Department for International Development (DFID) on partnerships in Brazil. This also brings to the fore questions of positioning. As Fowler (2000a; 2000b: 595) argues, NGOs/CSOs in developing countries need to carve out a space for themselves. In addition, donors should think carefully about the local political economy of aid. In a study of aid interfaces and the role of local elites in Nicaraguan rural villages, D'Exelle (2009: 1468) finds that 'village brokerage structures, as part of the interface with aid providers, are strongly correlated with recurrent exclusions from aid flows', and that the poorest are disproportionately affected. Pushing for political change – decentralising the brokerage structures – can thus be justified by its potential to reduce poverty.

Aid to MICs might entail supporting processes that have the potential to reduce rather than reinforce patterns of exclusion. This involves building long-term and consistent relationships with selected recipient organisations with social change agendas (e.g. local NGOs, community-based organisations, cooperatives etc.) (Eyben et al., 2004: 14), and gaining a deeper understanding of context. This means that aiding MICs becomes a fundamentally more political undertaking and, as such, donors will be required to involve themselves more intimately with domestic political processes, something they have tended to be unsure about doing – perhaps justifiably – in the past.

iii. Donor-MIC engagement to support the production and co-financing of global public goods

New interest in international or global public goods is fuelled, in part, by an understanding of globalisation and its impacts (Ferroni & Mody, 2002). Traditionally, donor assistance has not done much to increase the supply of global public goods (GPG) (Barrett, 2002). However, te Velde et al. (2002) find that donors with large aid budgets tend to be those that also have a larger share of GPG in their aid portfolios.

The main rationale behind providing GPGs is to regulate or compensate for the negative effects of global public 'bads', or 'products' which generate negative externalities across borders and reduce utility (Coyne & Ryan, 2008: 5), such as air pollution, civil war and violent conflict, disease, HIV/AIDS, international terrorism, and financial shocks.

According to Kaul et al. (1999: 2–3), GPGs must meet two key criteria. First, their benefits must have strong benefits of 'publicness' (i.e. they are characterised by non-rivalry in consumption and non-excludability).

Second, their benefits must be at least quasi-universal in terms of countries, people, and generations.

Meanwhile, Ferroni and Mody (2002: 1) argue more broadly that international public goods are primarily about three things: the rules that apply across borders; the institutions that supervise and enforce these rules; and the benefits that accrue without distinctions between countries (i.e. the (quasi) universality criterion noted above).

The provision of GPGs is particularly important not only because of the globalised nature of the contemporary world, but also because markets do not generally have sufficient incentives or the ability to allocate the necessary resources to public goods (Ferroni & Mody, 2002: 2). Governments too, when acting in isolation, are unable to provide them. Although GPGs can originate in both rich and developing countries – for example, while developing countries can contribute significantly towards climate change mitigation efforts, much funding for medical research, which feeds into health GPGs, is targeted in rich countries with the appropriate infrastructure (te Velde et al., 2002: 120) – their penetration, sustainability and impact hinge on negotiations and agreements at the global level. Barrett (2002: 73) points out that GPGs cannot usually be supplied by governments acting unilaterally; cooperation is typically needed. International organisations can play a key role in helping to build these relationships through their ability to convene; their ability to generate and transfer knowledge; and their ability to assist global and regional negotiations (Ferroni, 2001: 13).

Yet, Kaul et al. (1999: 450–1) argue that GPGs tend to be underprovided due to three 'gaps' within public policy making processes: a jurisdictional gap (i.e. the discrepancy between the global boundaries of major policy concerns and the national boundaries of policymaking); a participation gap (i.e. we live in a 'multi-actor' world but international cooperation remains primarily intergovernmental); and an incentive gap (i.e. there is not a strong enough case for countries to address their international spillovers or to cooperate on a GPG agenda). The (potential) supply of GPGs also takes place within an 'anarchic legal setting', making agreements at the international level difficult to thrash out (Barrett, 2002: 48). The successful supply of GPGs may rest on the resolution of conflicting interests at the national level. Combating climate change is arguably one of the most widely discussed examples of a GPG, but past summits and conferences (e.g. Kyoto) have only seen limited success.

GPGs are particularly important with respect to donor engagement with middle- income countries. Indeed, MICs themselves constitute key players in the supply of GPGs and forging and developing partnerships with MICs is increasingly important for global collective action. Engaging developmentally with MICs is thus seen as an end in itself (i.e. achieving poverty reduction in those countries), as well as a means to providing GPGs. We can therefore conceptualise GPGs in two ways: as a policy framework for engagement with MICs; and as fundamentally contingent on the actions and cooperation of MICs. Of particular relevance to the earlier discussion, Coyne and Ryan (2008) examine the possibility of foreign intervention in order to minimise global public 'bads' such as civil war (and the arguments could extend to global poverty). One could also note the parallel to the 'responsibility to protect' (R2P) in humanitarian assistance.

MICs are also central to the supply of regional public goods and, indeed, to the supply of regional public bads. For example, Fallon et al. (2001) describe how the spillover effects of the East Asian crisis affected the whole global economy and Rostoski (2006: 541) discusses the role of regional 'anchor countries' and 'locomotives', such as China, Indonesia and Thailand, claiming that cooperation with such countries produces positive effects for their neighbours.

Regional public goods are similar to GPGs; the main difference is spatial and scalar (although of course this also entails working within different legal and strategic frameworks). Kanbur (2001) distinguishes three kinds of activities to pursue regional public goods. First, non-country-specific investments in knowledge, dialogue, research into technologies, and negotiation of agreements on shared standards and policy regimes. Second, inter-country mechanisms for managing negative cross-border externalities and/or for creating beneficial ones. And third, country-specific action to take advantage of the benefits created under the two modalities above. The groundwork for pursuing regional public goods has arguably already been laid down in the shape of regional trade blocs and regional integration schemes.

Of relevance to the GPG discussion is the emergence of innovative finance. There is now an array of different sources of funding and aid channels. Innovative financing mechanisms (IFMs) and climate financing are two particular areas receiving increasing interest both in policy and academic arenas (see, for example, de Ferranti, 2006; Jones, 2010; Ketkar & Ratha, 2009; Lob-Levyt & Affolder, 2006; McCoy, 2009). There have been relatively few attempts to clarify an understanding of IFMs. As a recent NORAD (2009: 4) report notes, innovative financing means different things to different people and there is currently no exact overview of innovative financing flows.

What Does 'Aid 2.0' Look Like? 57

The following definition from Ketkar and Ratha (2009: 20), arguably, represents too narrow a classification:

> innovative financing involves risk mitigation and credit enhancement through the provision of collateral... spreading risk among many investors, and guarantees by higher-rated third parties.

Innovative financing certainly does have such characteristics, but it is not limited to these. Rather, IFMs mobilise previously un(der)utilised means of financing development-related initiatives, which differs in some way to the standard, 'traditional' system built on government/donor-recipient relationships.

Innovative financing is also about creating incentives for new actors to engage with development funding, often through set-ups based on market principles and closely involving private individuals, businesses and foundations. As one such example, (Product) RED is a means of financing the Global Fund through the licensing of its trademark to various companies (including Apple, American Express and Giorgio Armani). Owned by Bono and Bobby Shriver it 'provides a way for companies to tap into demand by so-called "conscience consumers" without having to develop their own brand... [C]ompanies can... make more money, and do good at the same time' (de Ferranti et al., 2008: 100).

A range of IFMs have been designed and implemented already, many of which relate to GPGs or at least regional, cross-border instruments and international or regional collaborations. Aside from some of the more well-known new institutional approaches to global health, such as the GAVI Alliance Fund, UNITAID is an initiative financed almost solely through airline ticket solidarity contributions. Other examples of innovative financing include: drug donation programs (Liese et al., 2010); Debt2Health (Taskforce on Innovative International Financing for Health Systems, 2009); the auction of greenhouse gas emissions permits (Taskforce on Innovative International Financing for Health Systems, 2009); and the Millennium Vaccine Initiative, which has channelled 1 billion USD in tax credits to corporations in order to promote delivery of existing vaccines and accelerate development of new vaccines for developing countries (Stansfield et al., 2002). On top of these there are also initiatives such as the International Health Partnership Plus (IHP+), which aims to strengthen national health systems, and Global Health Partnerships, for instance in Rwanda, which bring together reforms in financing with reforms in service delivery (Sandor, 2008).

Analysts point to the potentially huge revenues – for instance, 6–11bn USD from a tobacco tax in high-income countries (IFM Working Group 2, 2009) – as well as long-term sustainability of revenue flows and awareness raising. They also flag further benefits, from harmonisation of health systems flows (through a Health Systems Funding Platform) and increases in efficiency of private health sectors (through Seed Mechanisms), to double or even triple dividends associated with tobacco taxes and global environmental taxes (reducing the number of smoking-related diseases and reduced carbon emissions respectively). Relative to the range of IFMs already in place, the number of proposed options or options in the pipeline is substantial. Proposed initiatives also include procurement mechanisms whereby purchases of health products are pooled; mobile phone voluntary solidarity contributions; a global lottery endowment; and taxes on arms sales (Atkinson, 2005; de Ferranti *et al.*, 2008; Jha, 2004; Ratha *et al.*, 2008).

Climate financing is also likely to lead to a new generation of financing mechanisms. Brown (2009) outlines five categories of proposals, including the auctioning of assigned amount or emission allowances (rather than distribution for free to 'Annex I' domestic firms that have to comply with emissions reduction) and the creation of carbon market-based levies, such as the 2 per cent Clean Development Mechanism (CDM) levy which is used to raise funds for the Kyoto Protocol's Adaption Fund. Other proposals include imposing levies on international maritime transport and on air travel, developing a uniform global tax on CO_2 emissions (with a per capita exemption for least developed countries) and the issuance of bonds on international markets. These proposals are all means of creating new mechanisms to generate new and additional resources for addressing adaptation (and some mitigation activities) that are separate and additional to existing ODA (Brown *et al.*, 2010) and thus could be the basis for co-financing GPGs between donors and MICs.

iv. Donor-MIC engagement to support research and knowledge transfer/sharing

Over recent years there has been increasing interest in South-South cooperation and knowledge sharing among LICs and MICs. For example, the Task Team on South-South Cooperation put out a call for case stories on South-South knowledge exchange, stating that 'Low- and middle-income countries have achieved great knowledge in many areas, and practitioners around the world are discovering the power of exchanging their expertise' (Task Team on South-South Cooperation, 2011: 1). Further, the IEG evaluation of the World Bank's engagement in MICs, published in 2007 by the Independent Evaluation Group, states:

> The Bank has suggested that a justification for the level and comprehensiveness of its AAA [analytical and advisory activities] in MICs, and particularly in non-borrowing MICs, is the importance of deriving lessons that can be transferred to LICs. (IEG, 2007: 40)

The report also points out that one of the reasons why officials in Thailand and China continue to engage with the Bank is that they believe they have something to offer LICs, particularly those in the same region. This is illustrative of a wider point: knowledge sharing tends to be more prevalent within regions than between regions because of the transferability of knowledge across contexts (IEG, 2007: 40). The report also highlights a particular example of cross-country knowledge sharing – conditional cash transfer (CCT) programmes. Through interviews with staff, the report argues that the Bank had played a significant role in spreading new ideas regarding CCTs across countries. Methods for sharing included workshops, papers, publications, study tours, and events. However, while the Bank claims to aim to expose its staff to a range of developing countries so that they can 'bring experience from one MIC to another, and from MICs as a group to the LICs', the evaluation states it 'has proved difficult to find convincing data on this' (IEG, 2007: 40). In sum, from this perspective, donor engagement with MICs is understood as having an instrumental value – it enables donors to improve their developmental activities around the world, in both other MICs as well as in LICs.

What this discussion of new and alternative instruments ultimately suggests is that, in the future, aid to both LICs and MICs might look quite different from the traditional type of resource transfer currently associated for the most part with foreign aid. While in the remaining LICs peace and state-building may take an increasingly visible role, in MICs a 'beyond ODA' agenda is likely to be more appropriate.

Conclusions

Abstract: *Recapping the book's core arguments and messages, this concluding chapter clarifies in straightforward terms what the changing distribution of global poverty away from the poorest countries – the new geography of global poverty – means for the future of aid. In short, it re-emphasises the idea that what is required is a significant shift in the aid system from what might be termed 'Aid 1.0' (that is, aid as a resource transfer) towards 'Aid 2.0' (aid as global development cooperation).*

Sumner, Andy and Mallett, Richard. *The Future of Foreign Aid: Development Cooperation and the New Geography of Global Poverty.* Basingstoke: Palgrave Macmillan, 2013. DOI: 10.1057/9781137298881

There is a radically different context for international aid today than in the past – a context characterised by drastically fewer poor countries. Does this signal the end of aid for most countries, or a new kind of international cooperation? The discussion presented in this book suggests a significant shift in the aid system. Put crudely, this shift would be from 'Aid 1.0' (meaning aid defined largely as a resource transfer) to something different, perhaps an 'Aid 2.0'. This in turn suggests new principles and the need to genuinely reframe 'aid' as 'global development cooperation' (see Table C.1). 'Aid 1.0' has tended to be defined as follows: the 'problem' is poor people living in poor countries and the 'answer' is ODA resource transfers. In contrast, 'Aid 2.0' might be framed as follows: the 'problem' is that poverty is a 'global bad' and the 'answer' is that collective global action is needed. Further, the role of 'aid' in development would shift from being an external driver – filling gaps in a predictable and linear fashion – to support inclusive policy processes, co-financed GPGs, knowledge sharing/transfer and development policy coherence.

Following from this logic would be four principles for global development cooperation (GDC). First, that GDC be catalytic. This might mean a greater focus on opening up political/economic/media spaces and recognising that change is ultimately an internally-driven process that aid can play some limited role within. This would also point to 'aid to end aid' and the importance of domestic taxation systems.

Second, that GDC be based on a greater focus on risks/shocks/stressors and the use of global public goods to better deal with risk – indeed,

TABLE C.1 *'Aid 1.0' v. 'Aid 2.0': stylised characteristics*

	Aid 1.0 – 'Overseas Development Assistance' (ODA)	Aid 2.0 – 'Global Development Cooperation (GDC)'
The global poverty 'problem'	Poor people live in poor countries	Poverty as a 'global bad' – collective action needed
Aid policy responses	ODA resource transfer	Supporting inclusive policy processes, co-financing GPGs, knowledge sharing/transfer and development policy coherence
The nature of societal change	External drivers Predictable/linear interventions	Internally-driven 'Messy realities', 'edge of chaos'
The role of aid in development	Filling 'gaps'	Catalysing development

if many countries no longer need or want ODA then that money could be reallocated to global public goods. It is worth noting that even if "traditional aid" (meaning grants) is no longer in demand, concessional loans will still be useful even if grants are less appropriate given expanding resources.

Third, that GDC be based on research and knowledge transfer. This would not be a one-way transfer, but instead would be multiple in nature, with information flowing from MICs to LICs, from South to South, from South to North and so forth. Part of this principle requires noting that aid can help provide positive feedback loops via transparency and systems learning.

Fourth, that GDC be based on policy coherence across all policies related to global development, such as trade, migration and other key policy areas.

In sum, the changing distribution of global poverty away from the poorest countries to MICs suggests that a new approach is required. MICs will need and want 'traditional aid' less and less as domestic resources expand. However, concessional loans will still be useful even if grants are less appropriate given expanding resources.

In the foreseeable future there may be as few as 20 remaining LICs – most of which will be classified as fragile or conflict-affected and found in sub-Saharan Africa – and many MICs will no longer require ODA resource transfers. Indeed, many may be 'new' donors themselves (some already are). This changing dynamic necessitates a rethink of aid and a redesign of the aid system, and we have accordingly suggested a broad-based shift from resource transfers to global development cooperation. 'Aid 2.0' might provide us with a way of adapting to the new geography of global poverty.

Annex

TABLE A.1 *What determines aid 'effectiveness'? Selected cross-country studies*

Reference	Effectiveness for what?	Type of Study	Key Finding(s)/What Mediates Effectiveness?
Anderson and Waddington, 2007	Allocation strategies for poverty reduction	Econometric. Same countries used as Chen and Ravallion (2004), with the exception of Argentina, Sierra Leone, St Lucia, Slovenia.	Poverty-efficient aid allocations could lift 70 million people out of poverty by 2015.
Angeles and Neanidis, 2009	Economic growth	Econometric; growth-regression framework. Use dataset developed by Roodman (2004); covers 171 aid recipients over period 1958–2001.	The level of European settlement in colonial times is negatively related to the effectiveness of aid.
Baliamoune-Lutz and Mavrotas, 2009	Economic growth	Econometric. Use same dataset and similar methodology to Easterly *et al.* (2004), which is turn based on Burnside and Dollar (2000); data from 1970 to 1997.	Social capital and institutions enhance aid effectiveness; once accounted for, the impact of policy becomes statistically insignificant. Doubts raised over findings of Burnside and Dollar (2000).
Banerjee and Rondinelli, 2003	Privatisation	Econometric. Data on 35 countries; panel dataset of 630 observations from 1982–1999.	Aid has no systematic impact on the privatisation process. Privatisation is ultimately a domestic process. But aid, especially technical assistance, can positively affect the pace and intensity of privatisation; aid can be a facilitating factor in the presence of complementary institutional capacity.

Continued

TABLE A.1 Continued

Reference	Effectiveness for what?	Type of Study	Key Finding(s)/What Mediates Effectiveness?
Benarroch and Gaisford, 2004	Innovation and technology transfer	Econometric. Develop a dynamic Ricardian trade model with a continuum of goods; two kinds of aid considered (pure income transfers and aid that directly expedites technology transfer to South).	When aid is paid as a pure unilateral transfer, the conventional short-run terms-of-trade improvement that results from a home bias in consumption causes harmful delays in the transfer of technology that can lead to mutual immiserisation. Conversely, aid that directly or indirectly expedites technology transfer and learning in developing countries can be mutually beneficial.
Bjornskov, 2010	Income distribution	Exploration of data on income quintiles from World Income Inequality Database for 88 developing countries, 262 observations, 1960–2000.	Aid and democracy in conjunction are associated with a higher share of income held by the upper quintile (i.e. elites). Aid therefore leads to a more skewed income distribution in democratic developing countries, while the effects are negligible in autocratic countries.
Burnside and Dollar, 2000	Economic growth	Econometric. Use of modified neoclassical growth model and database developed by World Bank (56 countries, six four-year time periods from 1970–1973 until 1990–1993).	Aid has a positive impact on growth in developing countries with good fiscal, monetary and trade policies, but has little effect in the presence of poor policies. Aid would be more effective if it were more systemically conditioned on good policy.

Reference	Effectiveness for what?	Type of Study	Key Finding(s)/What Mediates Effectiveness?
Burnside and Dollar, 2004	Economic growth.	Econometric (dataset focusing on the 1990s, 124 countries); supplemented by case studies, project-level evidence and opinion polls.	Impact of aid depends on quality of state institutions and policies.
Chauvet and Guillaumont, 2009	Economic growth, exports volatility and income volatility	Econometric. Panel data for 87 countries, 1970–1999,	Aid makes growth more stable.
Collier and Dehn, 2001	Economic growth	Econometric. Annual data for 113 developing countries, 1957–1999.	Aid can be particularly important during periods characterised by a negative terms of trade shock.
Collier and Dollar, 2001; 2002	Economic growth	Econometric. Data from CPIA for 86 countries, 1974–1997.	'Poverty efficient' aid allocations: aid spending in accordance with recipient's economic policies and level of poverty. Aid effectiveness dependent on 'good' policy environment.
Collier and Hoeffler, 2002	Economic growth	Econometric. Dataset of large civil wars, covering 27 countries which were in their first decade of post-conflict economic recovery during the 1990s.	The effect of aid on growth is strongest between 4 and 7 years after the end of conflict.
Dalgaard et al., 2004	Productivity and growth	Econometric and theoretical. Use datasets from Burnside and Dollar (2000) and Easterly et al. (2003).	Aid has been effective in spurring growth, but the magnitude of the effect depends on climate-related circumstances.

Continued

TABLE A.1 Continued

Reference	Effectiveness for what?	Type of Study	Key Finding(s)/What Mediates Effectiveness?
Dollar and Easterly, 1999	Economic growth and policy change	Econometric.	Traditional aid-to-investment-growth linkages not very robust. Differences in economic policies can explain much of the differences in growth performances. Aid cannot easily promote lasting policy reform in countries in which there is no strong domestic movement in that direction – ownership more important than conditionality.
Doucouliagos and Paldam, 2009 (also Doucouliagos and Paldam, 2006; 2007; 2008)	Various	Review/meta-analysis of 97 aid effectiveness studies (up to 2005).	Aid has not been effective. There is a reluctance within the research community to publish negative results. Dutch disease provides a plausible explanation for the observed aid ineffectiveness.
Easterly, 2003	Economic growth	Critique of key studies, especially Burnside and Dollar.	The empirical links between aid and economic growth are far more fragile than Burnside and Dollar (2000) suggest. Definitions are very important (e.g. of 'aid', 'good policy', 'growth').
Easterly et al., 2003	Economic growth	Econometric. Same specification as Burnside and Dollar (2000), but with more data (sample covered 1970–1997).	Coefficient on interaction between aid and policy is insignificant: no support for conclusion that aid works in a good policy environment.

Reference	Effectiveness for what?	Type of Study	Key Finding(s)/What Mediates Effectiveness?
Feeny and McGillivray, 2009	Various	Econometric: 2004 panel data for 32 fragile and non-fragile states, drawn from OECD (2006) and World Bank (2006); data also from McGillivray and Feeny (2008).	Absorptive capacity constraints are important. Allocations should better reflect this. FCAS are diverse a group; analyses should take this into account.
Feeny and McGillivray, 2010	Economic growth	Econometric. Cross country annual data from 29 small island developing states (SIDS) for 1980–2004.	Aid is effective at spurring economic growth but with diminishing returns.
Gomanee et al., 2005b	Economic growth	Econometric. Data from 104 countries for 1980–2000, and for sub-samples of LICs and MICs.	Aid is associated with improved values of welfare indicators; this effect appears in be higher in LICs. Aid appears to increase welfare either directly or through effect on growth.
Guillaumont and Chauvet, 2001	Economic growth	Econometric. Data from 65 developing countries for two pooled 12-year periods.	The effects of aid on growth are not necessarily positive and depend on specific conditions in recipient. Aid effectiveness depends on exogenous environmental factors (e.g. terms of trade trend and real value of exports instability; climatic shocks)
Gyimah-Brempong et al., 2010	Economic growth	Econometric. Panel data from 77 developing countries (covering Africa, Asia, Middle East, Latin America and Caribbean), 1995–2004, two measures of aid, dynamic panel data estimator.	Relationship between aid and income growth is quadratic in nature. Negative partial growth effect of aid at low levels of aid, but positive effect when ratio of aid to GNI reaches threshold of between 6.6% and 14.4%. Positive and significant relationship between

Continued

TABLE A.1 Continued

Reference	Effectiveness for what?	Type of Study	Key Finding(s)/What Mediates Effectiveness?
			aid and physical capital investment. Accounting for indirect effects through investment, there is a positive growth effect at all levels of aid.
Hansen and Tarp, 2000	Economic growth	Survey of cross-country econometric literature on macroeconomic effectiveness of aid.	There is a robust aid-growth link.
Hermes and Lensink, 2001	Economic growth	Review of key aid effectiveness and selectivity literature.	Econometric evidence on macroeconomic effectiveness of aid is generally less convincing than has been claimed by the World Bank (1998). Good policies are context-specific.
Hudson and Mosley, 2001	Economic growth	Econometric. Annual data for wide sample of developing countries (all those with complete datasets for at least some years), 1969–1995.	Good policies appear to matter in stimulating growth, but do not appear to impact on aid effectiveness. Complex interaction between macroeconomic variables and good policies. Need to widen definition of good policies.
Karras, 2006	Economic growth	Econometric. Annual data from 71 aid-receiving developing economies for 1960–1997.	Effect of aid on economic growth is positive, permanent, statistically significant, and sizeable: raising aid by US$20/person of the recipient results in a permanent increase in growth rate of real GDP per capita by approximately 0.16%.

Reference	Effectiveness for what?	Type of Study	Key Finding(s)/What Mediates Effectiveness?
Kenny, 2008	Economic growth	Review of aid effectiveness literature.	Aid may have a role in promoting economic growth, but the exact mechanism is uncertain/too varied to identify. More work should investigate role of aid in promoting goals other than growth.
Khan and Hoshino, 1992	Various	Econometric. Sample of 5 South and Southeast Asian countries (India, Pakistan, Bangladesh, Sri Lanka, Malaysia), 1955–1976.	Aid affects consumption, investment and taxation of governments sampled, but relationship is a complex one. Grants and loans have different effects on investment and taxation.
Kosack, 2003	Quality of life	Econometric. Data from 46 countries for three four-year periods: 1974–1977; 1978–1981; 1982–1985). Aid data from World Bank; quality of life data from HDI; democratisation data from Polity IV and Freedom House.	Aid does not affect quality of life in the aggregate, but is effective when combined with democracy, and ineffective in autocracies.
Kosack and Tobin, 2006	Human development and economic growth.	Econometric: data from unbalanced panel of 103 countries (developing and developed), 1970–1999. Observations range from maximum of 363 over 90 countries to a minimum of 236 over 77 countries.	Aid contributes powerfully to both economic growth and human development; the higher the level of human capital in a country, the more aid contributes. Degree of democratic responsiveness does not appear to affect aid effectiveness. FDI does not have the same impacts and should not be used as a substitute for aid.

Continued

TABLE A.1 Continued

Reference	Effectiveness for what?	Type of Study	Key Finding(s)/What Mediates Effectiveness?
Lensink and White, 2000	Various	Critique of 'Assessing Aid' (World Bank 1998). Review of key studies.	Assessing Aid's growth regressions are not robust. The argument that aid only works when policies are right is not supported by other studies. The choice of which policies are good policies is problematic.
Loxley and Sackey, 2008	Economic growth	Econometric; fixed-effects growth models using pooled cross-section time series data from 40 AU member countries, 1973–2000.	Aid has a positive, statistically significant effect on investment and growth. Grant aid is more effective than other forms.
Markandya et al., 2010	Economic growth particularly long run	Econometric. Data from 95 developing countries, 1960–2000. Variables averaged over five time horizons: 1960–2000; 1960–1980; 1970–2000; 1980–2000; 1990–2000.	In long run, on average, aid volatility is negatively correlated with real economic growth. But relationship is not even: stronger for sub-Saharan African countries and not present in MICs or countries with strong institutions.
McGillivray, 2003	Economic growth	Survey of aid effectiveness and allocation.	Effectiveness of aid in increasing growth is contingent on a range of factors beyond quality of recipient policy regimes, including political stability, democracy, post conflict reconstruction, and economic vulnerability.
McGillivray et al., 2006	Economic growth	Survey of 50 years of empirical research on macroeconomic impact of aid (esp. on link between aid and growth).	Practically all research published since the World Bank's *Assessing Aid* agrees with the general finding that aid works

Reference	Effectiveness for what?	Type of Study	Key Finding(s)/What Mediates Effectiveness?
			to the extent that in its absence, growth would be lower. But many studies disagree with hypothesis that impact of aid on growth in contingent on recipient policy regimes.
Morrissey, 2001	Economic growth	Review of theoretical and empirical literature on links between aid and growth.	General picture is that aid contributes to investment and growth. Aid effectiveness appears greater when one tries to control for economic uncertainty.
Mosley and Suleiman, 2007	Economic growth and poverty reduction.	Econometric analysis (regressions). Data from pooled sample of 39 countries, 1980–2002. Case studies.	Composition and stability of aid matters for impact on poverty. Aid most effectively reduces poverty if it supports public expenditures which are supportive of agricultural development. Also true for education and infrastructure expenditures. Military expenditures have negative impact.
Mosley et al., 2004	Pro-poor public expenditure	Econometric. Data from pooled sample of 34 countries, 1980–2000 (and a 'pro-poor expenditure index')	Corruption, inequality and the composition of public expenditure all strongly associated with level of aid effectiveness. Aid allocations which take into account 'good micro and macro policies as well as income distribution and GDP per capita are more effective than ones which tend to ignore income distribution and the potential for impacting upon macroeconomic policies'. Aid can

Continued

TABLE A.1   Continued

Reference	Effectiveness for what?	Type of Study	Key Finding(s)/What Mediates Effectiveness?
Rajan and Subramanian, 2005	Economic growth	Econometric. Cross-sectional and panel data from 107 countries, 1960–2000.	Little robust evidence of a positive or negative relationship between aid inflows and economic growth. No evidence that that aid works better in better policy or geographical environments, or that certain forms of aid work better than others.
Ram, 2004	Economic growth	Econometric; the constraint of equality on the parameters of bilateral and multilateral aid is relaxed. Data primarily the same as Burnside and Dollar (2000): panel of six four-year averages from 1970–1973 to 1990–1993 for 56 aid-receiving LDCs (40 of which are LICs).	Little empirical evidence to support view that redirecting aid towards countries with 'good' policies leads to more growth and greater poverty reduction.
Robinson and Friedman, 2007	Policy engagement of domestic civil society organisations	Qualitative; comparative research in South Africa and Uganda. Data generated through in-depth studies of 12 organisations in RSA and Uganda; methods included interviews, focus groups, participant observation, document reviews.	Donor funding did not have a major effect on civil society policy engagement in either country. Donors can still provide logistical assistance (e.g. financial resources).

Reference	Effectiveness for what?	Type of Study	Key Finding(s)/What Mediates Effectiveness?
Roodman, 2004	Economic growth	Tests seven key aid-growth papers for robustness.	Fragility of results in the norm for aid effectiveness literature.
Suhrke and Buckmaster, 2006	Post-war peace	Quantitative and qualitative. Use civil war sample of Collier and Hoeffler – 14 countries and 17 post-conflict situations, 1971–1997 – but use annual figures rather than four-year averages and disaggregate aid. Then updated to 29 countries: 12 new and 10 old conflicts. Comparative case studies of 7 post-conflict cases.	High levels of post-war aid and rapid economic growth are not necessary preconditions for sustained post-war peace. Aid levels not clearly related to quality of peace, as measured by HDI.
Verschoor and Kalwij, 2006	Pro-poor growth; social indicators	Econometric. Data from 55 countries, 1980–1998.	Aid and recipient government's budget share allocated to social services tend to increase the size of the income elasticity of poverty and infant mortality; aid tends to increase this budget share.

References

Abegaz, B. (2005). 'Multilateral Development Aid for Africa'. *Economic Systems* 29: 433–54.

Abugre, C. (2000). *Still Sapping the Poor: A Critique of IMF Poverty Reduction Strategies*. London: World Development Movement.

Adams Jr., R. H. & Page, J. (2005). 'Do International Migration and Remittances Reduce Poverty in Developing Countries?'. *World Development* 33(10): 1645–69.

▶ ADB (2010). 'The rise of Asia's middle class'. In *Key Indicators for Asia and the Pacific 2010*. Mandaluyong City: ADB.

Addison, T., Mavrotas, G. & McGillivray, M. (2005). ' Aid, Debt Relief and New Sources of Finance for Meeting the Millennium Development Goals'. *Research Paper No. 2005/09*. Helsinki: UNU WIDER.

Agenor, P.-R., Bayraktar, N. & Aynaoui, K. E. (2008). 'Roads Out of Poverty? Assessing the Links between Aid, Public Investment, Growth, and Poverty Reduction'. *Journal of Development Economics* 86: 277–95.

Aldaba, F., Antezana, P., Valderrama, M. & Fowler, A. (2000). 'NGO Strategies beyond Aid: Perspectives from Central and South America and the Philippines'. *Third World Quarterly* 21(4): 669–83.

Aldenhoff, F.-O. (2007). 'Are Economic Forecasts of the International Monetary Fund Politically Biased? A Public Choice Analysis'. *Review of International Organizations* 2(3): 239–60.

Alesina, A. & Dollar, D. (2000). 'Who Gives Foreign Aid to Whom and Why?'. *Journal of Economic Growth* 5: 33–63.

Alkire, S., Roche, J., Santos, E. & Seth, S. (2011). *Multidimensional Poverty Index 2011*. Oxford: University of Oxford, Oxford Poverty & Human Development Initiative.

Amavilah, V. H. (1998). 'German Aid and Trade versus Namibian GDP and Labour Productivity'. *Applied Economics* 30(5): 689–95.

Anderson, E. & Waddington, H. (2007). 'Aid and the Millennium Development Goal Poverty Target: How Much is Required and How Should it be Allocated?'. *Oxford Development Studies* 35(1): 1–31.

Angeles, L. & Neanidis, K. C. (2009). 'Aid Effectiveness: The Role of the Local Elite'. *Journal of Development Economics* 90: 120–34.

Ansoms, A (2007). 'How Successful is the Rwandan PRSP? Growth, Poverty & Inequality'. *Review of African Political Economy* 34(112): 371–9.

Antman, F. & McKenzie, D. (2005). 'Poverty Traps and Nonlinear Income Dynamics with Measurement Error and Individual Heterogeneity'. *Policy Research Working Paper 3764*. Washington, DC: World Bank.

Anyanwu, J. C. & Erhijakpor, E. O. (2010). 'Do Remittances Affect Poverty in Africa?'. *African Development Review* 22(1): 51–91.

Arellano, C., Bulir, A., Lane, T. & Lipschitz, L. (2005). 'The Dynamic Implication of Foreign Aid and Its Variablity'. *Working Paper 05/119*. Washington, DC: International Monetary Fund.

Arvin, B. M. & Lew, B. (2010). 'Does Happiness Affect the Bilateral Aid Flows Between Donor and Recipient Countries?'. *European Journal of Development Research* 22: 546–63.

Atkinson, A. B. (ed.) (2005). *New Sources of Development Finance*. Oxford: Oxford University.

Azariadis, C. & Stachurski, J. (2005). 'Poverty Traps'. In Aghion, P. & Durlauf, S. N. (eds) *The Handbook of Economic Growth*. Amsterdam: Elsevier.

Baliamoune-Lutz, M. (2008). 'Institutions, Trade, and Social Cohesion in Fragile States'. *Working Paper 39*. Manchester: Brooks World Poverty Institute.

Baliamoune-Lutz, M. & Mavrotas, G. (2009). 'Aid Effectiveness: Looking at the Aid-Social Capital-Growth Nexus'. *Review of Development Economics* 13(3): 510–25.

Banerjee, A. & Duflo, E. (2008). 'What is Middle Class about the Middle Classes Around the World?'. *Journal of Economic Perspectives* 22(2): 3–28.

Banerjee, A. & He, R. (2003). 'Making Aid Work'. *Mimeo*. MIT.

Banerjee, S. G. & Rondinelli, D. A. (2003). 'Does Foreign Aid Promote Privatization? Empirical Evidence from Developing Countries'. *World Development* 31(9): 1527–

Barder, O. (2009a). 'Beyond Planning: Markets and Networks for Better Aid'. *Working Paper 185*. Washington, DC: Center for Global Development.

Barder, O. (2009b). 'What is Poverty Reduction?'. *Working paper 170*. Washington, DC: Center for Global Development.

Bardhan, P. (2001). 'Deliberative Conflicts, Collective Action, and Institutional Economics'. In Meier & Stiglitz (eds) *Frontiers of Development Economics*. New York, NY: Oxford University.

Barrett, S. (2002). 'Supplying International Public Goods: How Nations Can Cooperate'. In Ferroni, M. & Mody, A. (eds) *International Public Goods: Incentives, Measurement, and Financing*. Washington, DC: World Bank.

Batson, A., Meheus, F. & Brooke, S. (2006). 'Chapter 26: Innovative Financing Mechanisms to Accelerate the Introduction of HPV Vaccines in Developing Countries'. *Vaccine* 24 (Supplement 3): 219–25.

Bauer, P & Yamey, B. (1982). 'Foreign Aid: What is at Stake?'. Reprinted in Meier, G. M. (ed.) (1984) *Leading Issues in Economic Development*, Fourth Edition. Stanford, CA: Stanford University.

Baulch, B. (2006). 'Aid Distribution and the MDGs'. *World Development* 34(6): 933–50.

Benarroch, M. & Gaisford, J. D. (2004). 'Foreign Aid, Innovation, and Technology Transfer in a North-South Model with Learning-by-Doing'. *Review of Development Economics* 8(3): 361–78.

Berndt, E. R., Glennerster, R., Kremer, M. R., Lee, J., Levine, R., Weizsacker, G. & Williams, H. (2007). 'Advance Market Commitments for Vaccines against Neglected Diseases: Estimating Costs and Effectiveness'. *Health Economics* 16: 491–511.

Berthelemy, J-C. (2005). 'Bilateral donors' interest vs. recipients' development motives in aid allocation: do all donors behave the same?'. Paper presented at the HWWA Conference on the Political Economy of Aid, Hamburg, 9–11 December 2004.

Berthelemy, J-C. (2006a). 'Bilateral Donors' Interest vs. Recipients' Development Motives in Aid Allocation: Do All Donors Behave the Same?'. *Review of Development Economics* 10(2): 179–94.

Berthelemy, J-C. (2006b). 'Convergence and Development Traps: How Did Emerging Economies Escape the Underdevelopment Trap?'. In Bourguignon, F. & Pleskovic, B. (eds) *Growth and Integration: Annual World Bank Conference on Development Economics* pp. 127–56. Washington, DC: World Bank.

Berthelemy, J-C. & Tichit, A. (2002). 'Bilateral Donors' Aid Allocation Decisions: A Three-dimensional Panel Analysis'. *Discussion Paper 2002/123*. Helsinki: UNU-WIDER.

Berthelemy, J-C., Beuran, M. & Maurel, M. (2009). 'Aid and Migration: Substitutes or Complements?'. *World Development* 37(10): 1589–99.

Beynon, J. (2003). 'Poverty Efficient Aid Allocations – Collier/Dollar Revisited'. *ESAU Working Paper 2*. London: Overseas Development Institute.

Bird, G. (2010). 'The SDR Aid Link: It's Now or Never'. *Development Policy Review* 28(1): 63–74.

Birdsall, N. (2004). 'Seven Deadly Sins: Reflections on Donor Failings'. *Working Paper 50*. Washington, DC: Center for Global Development.

Birdsall, N. (2007). 'Do No Harm: Aid, Weak Institutions and the Missing Middle in Africa'. *Development Policy Review* 25(5): 575–98.

Birdsall, N (2010). 'The (indispensable) Middle Class in Developing Countries; or the Rich and the Rest, not the Poor and the Rest'. *Working Paper 207*. Washington, DC: CGD.

Birdsall, N, & Savedoff, W. (2010). 'Cash on Delivery: A New Approach to Foreign Aid'. Washington, DC: Center for Global Development.

Birdsall, N., Graham, C. & Pettinato, S. (2000). 'Stuck in the Tunnel: Is Globalization Muddling the Middle Class?'. *Working Paper 14*. Washington, DC: Center on Social and Economic Dynamics, Brookings Institution.

Birdsall, N., Rodrik, D. & Subramanian, A. (2005). 'How to Help Poor Countries'. *Foreign Affairs* 84(4): 136–52.

Bjornskov, C. (2010). 'Do Elites Benefit from Democracy and Foreign Aid in Developing Countries?'. *Journal of Development Economics* 92(2): 115–24.

Blomberg, S.B., Hess, G. D. & Thacker, S. (2000). 'Is there Evidence of a Poverty-Conflict Trap?'. Paper presented to a conference on The Economics of Political Violence, Centre of International Studies,

Woodrow Wilson School of Public and International Affairs, Princeton University, and the Development Research Group of the World Bank, 18–19 March.

Boone, P. (1996). 'Politics and the Effectiveness of foreign aid'. *European Economic Review* 40: 289–329.

Booth, D. (2003). 'Introduction and Overview'. *Development Policy Review* 21(2): 131–59.

Booth, D. (2011). 'Aid, Institutions and Governance: What Have We Learned?'. *Development Policy Review* 29(S1): 5–26.

Bourguignon, F. & da Silva, L. (2001). 'Evaluating the Poverty and Distributional Impact of Economic Policies: A Compendium of Existing Techniques'. In Bourguignon, F. & da Silva, L. (eds) *The Impact of Economic Policies on Poverty and Income Distribution*, pp. 1–26. Oxford and New York, NY: Oxford University.

Bourguignon, F. & Sundberg, M. (2007). 'Aid Effectiveness – Opening the Black Box'. *AEA Papers and Proceedings* 97(2): 316–21.

Branchflower, A., Hennell, S., Pongracz, S. & Smart, M. (2004). 'How Important are Difficult Environments to Achieving the MDGs?'. *PRDE Working Paper 2*. London: Poverty Reduction in Difficult Environments Team, Policy Division, DFID.

Brown, D. (2004). 'Participation in Poverty Reduction Strategies: Democracy Strengthened or Democracy Undermined?'. In Hickey, S. & Mohan, G. (eds) *Participation: From Tyranny to Transformation?* London: Zed.

Brown, G. & Stewart, F. (2006). 'The Implications of Horizontal Inequality for Aid'. *CRISE Working Paper 36*. Oxford: CRISE, University of Oxford.

Brown, J. (2009). 'Carbon Finance in Africa'. Prepared for Special Session on Climate Change, Addis Ababa, 3 September.

Brown, J., Cantore, N. & te Velde, D. W. (2010). 'Climate Financing and Development: Friends or Foes?'. Paper commissioned by The ONE Campaign. London: ODI.

Burnside, C. & Dollar, D. (2000). 'Aid, Policies and Growth'. *American Economic Review* 90(4): 847–68.

Burnside, C. & Dollar, D. (2004). 'Aid, Policies and Growth: Revisiting the Evidence'. *Policy Research Paper O-2834*. Washington, DC: World Bank.

Cammack, D., McLeod, D., Rocha Menocal, A. & Christiansen, K. (2006). 'Donors and the "Fragile States" Agenda: A Survey of Current Thinking and Practice'. Report submitted to JICA. London: ODI.

CGD (Centre for Global Devlopment) (2012). 'Commitment to Development Index'. http://www.cgdev.org/section/initiatives/_active/cdi/ Accessed 1 April 2011.

Chandy, L. & Gertz, G. (2011). 'Poverty in Numbers: The Changing State of Global Poverty from 2005 to 2015'. *Policy brief 2011-01*. Washington, DC: Global Economy and Development at Brookings, Brookings Institution.

Chang, H-J. (2002). *Kicking Away the Ladder: Development Strategy in Historical Perspective*. London: Anthem.

Chatterjee, S. & Turnovsky, S. J. (2005). 'Financing Public Investment through Foreign Aid: Consequences for Economic Growth and Welfare'. *Review of International Economics* 13(1): 20–44.

Chauvet, L. & Guillaumont, P. (2009). 'Aid, Volatility, and Growth Again: When Aid Volatility Matters and When it Does Not'. *Review of Development Economics* 13(3): 452–63.

Chen, S. & Ravallion, M. (2004) 'How Have the World's Poorest Fared Since the Early 1980s?', World Bank Research Observer, 19(2): 141-170.

Chen, S. & Ravallion, M. (2008). 'The Developing World is Poorer than thought but no Less Successful in the Fight against Poverty'. *Policy Research Working Paper 4703*. Washington, DC: World Bank.

Chenery, H.B. & Eckstein, P. (1970). 'Development Alternatives for Latin America'. *Journal of Political Economy* 78(4): 966–1006.

Chenery, H.B. & Strout, A.M. (1966). 'Foreign Assistance and Economic Development'. *American Economic Review* 56(4): 679–733.

CIDSE (2005). 'New Resources for Development'. *CIDSE Position Paper*. CIDSE.

Clemens, M. A., Kenny, C. J. & Moss, T. J. (2007). 'The Trouble with the MDGs: Confronting Expectations of Aid and Development Success'. *World Development* 35(5): 735–51.

Clemens, M., Radelet, S. & Bhavani, R. (2004). 'Counting Chickens when they Hatch: The Short-Term Effect of Aid on Growth'. *Working Paper 44*. Washington, DC: Center for Global Development.

Clist, P. (2009). '25 Years of Aid Allocation Practice: Comparing Donors and Eras'. *CREDIT research paper 09/11*. Nottingham: Centre for Research in Economic Development and International Trade, University of Nottingham.

Clist, P. & Morrissey, O. (2009). 'Aid and Tax Revenue: Signs of a Positive Effect Since the 1980s'. *Journal of International Development*.

CODE (Committee on Development Effectiveness) (n.d.). 'CODE Chairman's Summary'. http://web.worldbank.org/WBSITE/EXTERNAL/EXTOED/EXTMIDINCCOUN/0,,contentMDK:21398641~menuPK:5006333~pagePK:64829573~piPK:64829550~theSitePK:4434098,00.html Accessed 1 April 2011.

Collier, P. (2007). *The Bottom Billion: Why the Poorest Countries are Failing and What Can be Done About It.* Oxford: Oxford University.

Collier, P. & Dehn, J. (2001). 'Aid, Shocks, and Growth'. *Working Paper 2688.* Washington, DC: World Bank.

Collier, P. & Dollar, D. (2001). 'Can the World Cut Poverty in Half? How Policy Reform and Effective Aid Can Meet International Development Goals'. *World Development* 29(11): 1787–802.

Collier, P. & Dollar, D. (2002). 'Aid Allocation and Poverty Reduction'. *European Economic Review* 46(8)L 1475–500.

Collier, P. & Hoeffler, A. (2004). 'Aid, Policy and Growth in Post-conflict Societies'. *European Economic Review* 48(5): 1125–45.

Collier, P., Elliott, V. L., Hegre, H., Hoeffler, A., Reynal-Querol, M. & Sambanis, N. (2003). *Breaking the Conflict Trap: Civil War and Development Policy.* Washington, DC: World Bank.

Cordero, C. et al. (2008). 'Funding Agencies in Low- and Middle-income Countries: Support for Knowledge Translation'. *Bulletin of the World Health Organisation* 86: 524–34.

Coyne, C. J. & Ryan, M. E. (2008). 'Foreign Intervention and Global Public Bads'. *Mimeo.*

Cramer, C. & Goodhand, J. (2002). 'Try Again, Fail Again, Fail Better? War, the State, and the "Post-Conflict" Challenge in Afghanistan'. *Development and Change* 33(5): 885–909.

Dalgaard, C.-J. & Hansen, H. (2001). 'On Aid, Growth and Good Policies'. *Journal of Development Studies* 37(6): 17–35.

Dalgaard, C-J., Hansen, H. & Tarp, F. (2004). 'On the Empirics of Foreign Aid and Growth'. *Economic Journal* 114(496): 191–216.

Dawson, P. J. & Tiffin, R. (1999). 'Is There a Long-run Relationship between ODA and GDP? The Case of India'. *Applied Economics Letters* 6(5): 275–77.

Deaton, A. (2010). 'Price Indexes, Inequality, and the Measurement of World Poverty'. *American Economic Review* 100(1): 5–34.

Deaton, A. & Heston, A. (2010). 'Understanding PPPs and PPP-based National Accounts'. *American Economic Journal* 2(4): 1–35.

de Ferranti, D. M. (2006). 'Innovative Financing Options and the Fight Against Global Poverty: What's New and What's Next?'. Washington, DC: Brookings Institution.

de Ferranti, D., Griffin, C., Escobar, M. L., Glassman, A. & Lagomarsino, G. (2008). 'Innovative Financing for Global Health: Tools for Analyzing the Options'. *Working Paper 2*. Washington, DC: Global Health Financing Initiative, Brookings Institution.

Demekas, D. G., McHugh, J. & Kosma, T. (2002). 'The Economics of Post Conflict Aid'. *Working Paper 02/198*. Washington, DC: IMF.

Desai, R. M. & Kharas, H. (2008). 'The California Consensus: Can Private Aid End Global Poverty?'. *Survival* 50(4): 155–68.

Deutsche Bank (2009). 'Emerging Asia's Middle Class: A Force to be Reckoned with'. *Current Issues, Deutsche Bank Research*. Frankfurt: Deutsche Bank.

Devarajan, S., Easterly,W. & Pack, H. (2004). 'Low Investment Is Not the Constraint on African Development'. *Economic Development and Cultural Change* 51: 547–71.

Devarajan, S., Ehrhart, H., Minh Le, T. & Raballand, G. (2011). 'Direct Redistribution, Taxation, and Accountability in Oil-Rich Economies: A Proposal'. *Working Paper 281*. Washington, DC: Center for Global Development.

Develtere, P. & De Bruyn, T. (2009). 'The Emergence of a Fourth Pillar in Development Aid'. *Development in Practice* 19(7): 912–22.

Devereux, S. (2006). 'Cash Transfers and Social Protection'. Paper prepared for 'Cash transfer activities in southern Africa' regional workshop, Johannesburg, 9–10 October.

D'Exelle, B. (2009). 'Excluded Again: Village Politics at the Aid Interface'. *Journal of International Development Studies* 45(9): 1453–71.

DFID (2005). 'Review of DFID's Drivers of Change Country Study Reports'. London: DFID.

Dijkstra, G. (2005). 'The PRSP Approach and the Illusion of Improved Aid Effectiveness: Lessons from Bolivia, Honduras and Nicaragua'. *Development Policy Review* 23(4): 443–64.

Djankov, S., Montalvo, J. G., & Reynal-Querol, M. (2009). 'Aid with Multiple Personalities'. *Journal of Comparative Economics* 37: 217–29.

Dollar, D. & Collier, P. (1999). 'Aid Allocation and Poverty Reduction'. Policy Research Working Paper 2041. Washington, DC: World Bank.

Dollar, D. & Easterly, W. (1999). 'The Search for the Key: Aid, Investment and Policies in Africa'. *Journal of African Economies* 8(4): 546–77.

Dollar, D. & Levin, V. (2004). 'The Increasing Selectivity of Foreign Aid, 1984–2002'. *Policy Research Working Paper 3299*. Washington, DC: World Bank.

Doucouliagos, H. & Paldam, M. (2006). 'Aid Effectiveness on Accumulation. A Meta-study'. *Kyklos* 59: 227–54.

Doucouliagos, H. & Paldam, M. (2007). 'Conditional Aid Effectiveness. A Meta-study'. *Working Paper 2005-14*. School of Economics and Management, Aarhus University.

Doucouliagos, H. & Paldam, M. (2008). 'Aid Effectiveness on Growth. A Meta-study'. *European Journal of Political Economy* 24: 1–24.

Doucouliagos, H. & Paldam, M. (2009). 'The Aid Effectiveness Literature: The Sad Results of 40 Years of Research'. *Journal of Economic Surveys* 23(3): 433–61.

Dudley, L. & Montmarquette, C. (1976). 'A Model of the Supply of Bilateral Foreign Aid'. *American Economic Review* 66(1): 132–42.

Duponchel, M. (2008). 'Can aid break the conflict trap?'. Paper presented at the Centre for the Study of African Economies Conference 2008, Economic Development in Africa. Oxford, 16–18 March.

Easterly, W. (2002). 'The Cartel of Good Intentions: Bureaucracy vs. Markets in Foreign Aid'. *Working Paper 4*. Washington, DC: Center for Global Development.

Easterly, W. (2003). 'Can Foreign Aid buy Growth?'. *Journal of Economic Perspectives*, 17: 23–48.

Easterly, W. (2006). *The White Man's Burden: Why the West's Efforts to Aid the Rest have done so much Ill and so Little Good*. New York, NY: Penguin.

Easterly, W., Levine, R. & Roodman, D. (2003). 'New Data, New Doubts: Revisiting "Aid, Policies, and Growth"'. *Working Paper 26*. Washington, DC: Center for Global Development.

ECOSOC (2008). 'Background Study for the Development Cooperation Forum – Trends in South-South and Triangular Development Cooperation'. New York, NY: United Nations.

Edgren, G. (2002). 'Aid is an Unreliable Joystick'. *Development and Change* 33(2): 261–67.

Elbadawi, I. A., Kaltani, L. & Schmidt-Hebbel, K. (2007). 'Post-Conflict Aid, Real Exchange Rate Adjustment, and Catch-up Growth'. *Working Paper 4187*. Washington, DC: World Bank.

ERD (2009). *Overcoming Fragility in Africa*. San Domenico di Fiesole: Robert Schuman Centre for Advanced Studies, European University Institute.

Eubank, N. (2010). 'Peace-Building without External Assistance: Lessons from Somaliland'. *Working Paper 198*. Washington, DC.: Center for Global Development.

Evans, A. (2010). *Aid Effectiveness Post-2010 – A Think Piece on Ways Forward*. London: Overseas Development Institute.

Evans, P. (2004). 'Development as Institutional Change: The Pitfalls of Monocropping and the Potentials of Deliberation'. *Studies in Comparative International Development* 38(4): 30–52.

Eyben, R. & Lister, S. with Dickinson, B., Olivie, I. & Tejada, L. (2004). 'Why and how to aid "Middle Income Countries"'. *Working Paper 231*. Brighton: IDS.

Eyben, R., Kidder, T., Rowlands, J. & Bronstein, A. (2008). 'Thinking about Change for Development Practice: A Case Study from Oxfam GB'. *Development in Practice* 18(2): 201–12.

Faini, R. (2006). 'Trade Liberalization in a Globalizing World'. In Bourguignon, F. & Pleskovic, B. (eds) *Growth and Integration: Annual World Bank Conference on Development Economics* pp. 195–222. Washington, DC: World Bank.

Fallon, P., Hon, V., Qureshi, Z. & Ratha, D. (2001). *Middle Income Countries: Development Challenges and Growing Global Role*. Washington, DC: World Bank.

Feeny, S. (2005). 'The Impact of Foreign Aid on Economic Growth in Papua New Guinea'. *Journal of Development Studies* 41(6): 1092–1117.

Feeny, S. & McGillivray, M. (2008). 'Scaling up Foreign Aid: Will the Big Push Work?'. Mimeo. Melbourne: RMIT University.

Feeny, S. & McGillivray, M. (2009). 'Aid Allocation to Fragile States: Absorptive Capacity Constraints'. *Journal of International Development* 21: 618–32.

Feeny, S. & McGillivray, M. (2010). 'Aid and Growth in Small Island Developing States'. *Journal of Development Studies* 46(5): 897–917.

Fenton, N. (2008). 'International Finance: Aid and Middle-Income Countries'. *From Poverty to Power Background Paper*. Oxford: Oxfam.

Ferroni, M. (2001). 'Regional Public Goods in Official Development Assistance'. *Occasional Paper 11*. Buenos-Aires: Inter-American Development Bank.

Ferroni, M. & Mody, A. (2002). 'Global Incentives for International Public Goods: Introduction and Overview'. In Ferroni, M. & Mody, A. (eds) *International Public Goods: Incentives, Measurement, and Financing*. Washington, DC: World Bank.

Ffrench-Davis, R. (2009). 'The Global Crisis, Speculative Capital and Innovative Financing for Development'. *CEPAL Review* 97: 57–74.

Fink, G. & Redaelli, S. (2010). 'Determinants of International Emergency Aid – Humanitarian Need Only?'. *World Development*, article in press.

Fioramonti, L. (2008). 'Micro-Assistance to Democracy and Sustainability: An Empirical Study of EU Aid to Post-Apartheid South Africa'. *Politikon* 35(3): 321–38.

Fischer, A. M. (2009). 'Putting Aid In Its Place: Insights From Early Structuralists on Aid and Balance of Payments and Lessons for Contemporary Aid Debates'. *Journal of International Development* 21: 856–67.

Fischer, A. (2010). 'Towards Genuine Universalism within Contemporary Development Policy'. *IDS Bulletin* 41(1): 36–44.

Fleck, R. F. & Kilby, C. (2006). 'How Do Political Changes Influence US Bilateral Aid Allocations? Evidence from Panel Data'. *Review of Development Economics* 10(2): 210–23.

Foster, M. (2000). 'New Approaches to Development Co-operation: What can we Learn from Experience with implementing Sector Wide Approaches?'. *Working Paper 140*. London: Overseas Development Institute.

Foster, M. & Leavy, J. (2001) 'The Choice of Financial Aid Instruments'. *Working Paper 158*. London: Overseas Development Institute.

Forster, J. & Stokke, O. (1999). 'Coherence of Policies Towards Developing Countries: Approaching the Problematique'. In Forster, J. & Stokke, O. (eds) *Policy Coherence in Development Co-operation*. London: Frank Cass.

Fowler, A. (2000a). 'NGDOs as a Moment in History: Beyond Aid to Social Entrepreneurship or Civic Innovation?'. *Third World Quarterly* 21(4): 637–54.

Fowler, A. (2000b). 'NGO Futures: Beyond Aid: NGDO Values and the Fourth Position'. *Third World Quarterly* 21(4): 589–603.

Frantz, T. R. (1987). 'The Role of NGOs in the Strengthening of Civil Society'. *World Development* 15(S1): 121–27.

Fraser, A. (2005). 'Poverty Reduction Strategy Papers: Now who calls the Shots?'. *Review of African Political Economy* 32(104): 317–40.

Gillies, D. (1999). *Between Principle and Practice. Human Rights in North-South Relations*. Montreal: McGill-Queen's University Press.

Giovannetti, G. (2010). *Social Protection for Inclusive Development: A New Perspective in EU Co-operation with Africa*. European Report on Development. San Domenico di Fiesole: European University Institute.

Girishankar, N. (2009). 'Innovating Development Finance: From Financing Source to Financial Solutions'. *CFP Working Paper Series No. 1*. Washington, DC: CFP, World Bank.

Glassman, A., Duran, D. & Sumner, A. (2011). 'Global Health and the New Bottom Billion: What Do Shifts in Global Poverty and the Global Disease Burden Mean for GAVI and the Global Fund?'. *Working Paper 270*. Washington, DC: Center for Global Development.

Gomanee, K., Girma, S. & Morrissey, O. (2005a). 'Aid and Growth in Sub-Saharan Africa: Accounting for Transmission Mechanisms'. *Journal of International Development* 17(8): 1055–75.

Gomanee, K., Morrissey, O., Mosley, P. & Verschoor, A. (2005b). 'Aid, Government Expenditure, and Aggregate Welfare'. *World Development* 33(3): 355–70.

Green, D. (2008). *From Poverty to Power: How Active Citizens and Effective States Can Change the World*. Oxford: Oxfam.

Griffin, K. (1970). 'Foreign Capital, Domestic Savings and Economic Development'. *Bulletin of the Oxford University Institute of Economics and Statisitcs* 32: 99–112.

Grindle, M. S. (2004). 'Good Enough Governance: Poverty Reduction and Reform in Developing Countries'. *Governance: An International Journal of Policy, Administration and Institutions* 17: 525–48.

Grindle, M. S. (2007). 'Good Enough Governance Revisited'. *Development Policy Review* 25(5): 553–74.

Guillaumont, P. & Chauvet, L. (2001). 'Aid and Performance: A Reassessment'. *Journal of Development Studies* 37(6): 66–92.

Gyimah-Brempong, K., Racine, J. S. & Gyapong, A. (2010). 'Aid and Economic Growth: Sensitivity Analysis'. *Journal of International Development*.

Hadenius, A. & Uggla, F. (1996). 'Making Civil Society Work, Promoting Democratic Development: What can States and Donors do?'. *World Development* 24(10): 1621–39.

Hadjimichael, M. T., Ghura, D., Muhleisen, M., Nord, R. & Murat Ucer, E. (1995). 'Sub-Saharan Africa: Growth, Savings, and Investment 1986–93'. *Occasional Paper 118*. Washington, DC: International Monetary Fund.

Hansen, H. & Tarp, F. (2000). 'Aid Effectiveness Disputed'. *Journal of International Development* 12: 547–70.

Hansen, H. & Tarp, F. (2001). 'Aid and Growth Regressions'. *Journal of Development Economics* 64: 547–70.

Harttgen, K and Klasen, S. (2010). 'Fragility and MDG Progress: How Useful is the Fragility Concept?'. *European University Institute Working Paper 2010/20*. Robert Schuman Centre For Advanced Studies.

Harvey, P., Holmes, R., Slater, R. & Martin, E. (2007). 'Social Protection in Fragile States'. *Final Report*. London: Overseas Development Institute.

Hattori, T. (2001). 'Reconceptualizing Foreign Aid'. *Review of International Political Economy* 8(4): 633–60.

Hayman, R. (2009). 'From Rome to Accra via Kigali: "Aid Effectiveness" in Rwanda'. *Development Policy Review* 27(5): 581–99.

Hayter, T. (1971). *Aid as Imperialism*. Harmondsworth: Penguin.

Hayter, T. & Watson, C. (1985). *Aid: Rhetoric and Reality*. London: Pluto.

Hearn, J. (1999). 'Foreign Aid, Democratisation and Civil Society in Africa: A Study of South Africa, Ghana and Uganda'. *Discussion Paper 368*. Brighton: IDS.

Heller, P. S. & Gupta, S. (2004). 'More Aid – Making It Work for the Poor'. In Gupta, S., Clements, B. & Inchauste, G. (eds) *Helping Countries Develop: The Role of Fiscal Policy*, pp. 407–21. Washington, DC: International Monetary Fund.

Heltberg, R. (2002). 'The Poverty Elasticity of Growth'. *Discussion Paper 2002/21*. Helsinki: UNU-WIDER.

Hermes, N. & Lensink, R. (2001). 'Changing the Conditions for Development Aid: A New Paradigm?'. *Journal of Development Studies* 37(6): 1–16.

Hobley, M. (2003) 'Workshop Report – Partnership and Influencing Workshop'. São Paolo, Brazil: DFID.

Hoekman, B. & Nicita, A. (2010). 'Assessing the Doha Round: Market Access, Transactions Costs and Aid for Trade Facilitation'. *Journal of International Trade and Economic Development* 19(1): 65–79.

Holmes, R., Jones, N., Vargas, R. & Veras, F. (2010). 'Cash Transfers and Gendered Risks and Vulnerabilities: Lessons from Latin America'. *Background Note*, October 2010. London: ODI.

Howell, J. (2000). 'Making Civil Society from the Outside: Challenges for Donors'. *European Journal of Development Research* 12(1): 3–22.

Howell, J. & Pearce, J. (2000). 'Civil Society: Technical Instrument or Social Force for Change?'. In D. Lewis and T. Wallace (eds) *New Roles and Relevance: Development NGOs and the Challenge of Change*, pp. 75–87. Bloomfield: Kumarian.

Howes, S. (2011). 'An Overview of Aid Effectiveness Determinants and Strategies'. *Discussion Paper 1*. Canberra: Development Policy Centre, Australian National University.

Hudson, J. & Mosley, P. (2001). 'Aid Policies and Growth: In Search of the Holy Grail'. *Journal of International Development* 13: 1023–38.

I-8 (2009). *Innovative Financing for Development*. New York, NY: United Nations.

IAVI (2009). 'Innovative Financing Mechanisms To Advance Global Health'. *Policy Brief 21*. IAVI Insights.

IEG (2007). *Development Results in Middle-Income Countries: An Evaluation of the World Bank's Support*. Washington, DC: The Independent Evaluation Group, World Bank.

IFAD (2010). 'IFAD's Engagement with Middle-Income Countries'. Evaluation Committee, 65th Session, Rome, 25–26 November.

Islam, M. (2003). 'Political Regimes and the Effects of Foreign Aid on Economic Growth'. *Journal of Developing Areas* 37: 35–53.

Jaradat, R. (2008). 'The impact of donor and recipient government policies and practices on the effectiveness of foreign aid to a middle income developing country: case studies from Jordan'. *Doctoral thesis*. University of Huddersfield.

Jha, R. (2004). 'Innovative Sources of Development Finance: Global Cooperation in the Twenty-first Century'. *World Economy* 27: 193–214.

Jones, B. & Chandran, R. with Cousens, E., Slotin, J. & Sherman, J. (2008). 'Concepts and Dilemmas of Statebuilding in Fragile Situations: From Fragility to Resilience'. *OECD/DAC Discussion Paper*. Paris: OECD.

Jones, N. & Walsh, C. (2008). 'Policy briefs as a communication tool for development research'. *Background Note*, May 2008. London: ODI.

Jones, N., Datta, A. & Jones, H. with ebpdn partners (2009). *Knowledge, Policy and Power: Six Dimensions of the Knowledge-Development Policy Interface.* London: ODI.

Jones, S. (2009). 'Alternative Development Financing Mechanisms: Pre-Crisis Trends and Post-Crisis Outlook'. *DIIS Report 11.* Copenhagen: Danish Institute for International Studies.

Jones, S. (2010). 'Innovating Foreign Aid – Progress and Problems'. *Journal of International Development.*

Kanbur, R. (2001). 'Cross-Border Externalities, International Public Goods and Their Implications for Aid Agencies'. *Working Paper 2001–03.* Ithaca, NY: Cornell University.

Kanbur, R. (2003) The Economics of International Aid. Downloaded at: http://www.arts.cornell.edu/poverty/kanbur/handbookaid.pdf

Kanbur, R. & Mukherjee, D. (2007). 'Poverty, Relative to the Ability to Eradicate it: An Index of Poverty Reduction Failure'. *Working paper 2007–02.* Ithaca, NY: Charles H. Dyson School of Applied Economics and Management, Cornell University.

Kanbur, R. & Sumner, A. (2011). 'Poor Countries or Poor People? Development Assistance and the New Geography of Global Poverty'. *Working Paper 2011–08.* Ithaca, NY: Charles H. Dyson School of Applied Economics and Management, Cornell University.

Kapstein, E. B. (2005). 'The Politics of Policy Coherence'. In *Fostering Development in a Global Economy: A Whole of Government Perspective.* Paris: OECD.

Karras, G. (2006). 'Foreign Aid and Long-Run Economic Growth: Empirical Evidence for a Panel of Developing Countries'. *Journal of International Development* 18: 15–28.

Karver, J., Kenny, C. & Sumner, A. (2012). 'MDGs 2.0: What Goals, Targets, and Timeframe?'. *Working Paper 297.* Washington, DC: Center for Global Development.

Katseli, L. T., Lucas, R. E. B. & Xenogiani, T. (2006). 'Effects of Migration on Sending Countries: What Do We Know?'. *Working Paper 250.* Paris: OECD Development Centre, OECD.

Kaul, I., Grunberg, I. & Stern, M. A. (1999). 'Defining Global Public Goods'. In Kaul, I., Grunberg, I. & Stern, M. A. (eds) *Global Public Goods: International Cooperation in the 21st Century.* New York, NY: UNDP.

Kenny, C. (2008). 'What is Effective Aid? How Would Donors Allocate it?'. *European Journal of Development Research* 20(2): 330–46.

Kenny, C. & Williams, D. (2001). 'What Do We Know About Economic Growth? Or, Why Don't We Know Very Much?'. *World Development* 29(1): 1-22.

Ketkar, S. & Ratha, D. (2009). *Innovative Financing for Development*. Washington, DC: World Bank.

Khan, H. A. & Hoshino, E. (1992). 'Impact of Foreign Aid on the Fiscal Behavior of LDC Governments'. *World Development* 20(10): 1481–88.

Kharas, H. (2007). *The New Reality of Aid*. New York, NY: Brookings Blum Roundtable.

Kharas, H. (2008). 'Measuring the Cost of Aid Volatility'. *Working Paper 3*. Washintgon, DC: Wolfensohn Center for Development at Brookings.

Kharas, H. (2010). 'The Emerging Middle Class in Developing Countries'. *Working Paper 285*. Paris: OECD Development Centre.

Kharas, H. & Rogerson, A. (2012). *Horizon 2025: Creative Destruction in the Aid Industry*. London: Overseas Development Institute.

Killick, T. & Foster, M. (2011). 'The Macroeconomics of Doubling Aid to Africa and the Centrality of the Supply Side'. *Development Policy Review* 29(S1): 83–108.

Klasen, S. (2010). 'Levels and trends in absolute poverty in the world: what we know and what we don't'. Paper prepared for the International Association for Research in Income and Wealth, St. Gallen, Switzerland, August 22–28.

Klein, M. & Harford, T. (2005a). *The Market for Aid*. Washington, DC: IFC.

Klein, M. & Harford, T. (2005b). 'Grants or Loans? Development Finance and Incentive Effects'. Public Policy for the Private Sector Note 287.

Knack, S. & Rahman, A. (2004). 'Donor Fragmentation and Bureaucratic Quality in Aid Recipients'. *Policy Research Working Paper 3186*. Washington, DC: World Bank.

Koch, D-J., Dreher, A., Nunnenkamp, P. & Thiele, R. (2009). 'Keeping a Low Profile: What Determines the Allocation of Aid by Non-Governmental Organisations?'. *World Development* 37(5): 902–18.

Kosack, S. (2003). 'Effective Aid: How Democracy Allows Development Aid to Improve the Quality of Life'. *World Development* 31(1): 1–22.

Kosack, S. & Tobin, J. (2006). 'Funding Self-Sustaining Development: The Role of Aid, FDI and Government in Economic Success'. *International Organisation* 60: 205–43.

Künnemann, R. & Leonhard, R. (2008). *A Human Rights View of Social Cash Transfers for Achieving the Millennium Development Goals*. Bonn / Stuttgart: Brot für die Welt, Evangelischer Entwicklungsdienst, FIAN International, medico international.

Larbi-Jones, E. (2004). 'Working for Pro-poor Change in Brazil: Influencing Partnerships?'. *Lessons for Change in Policy and Organisations 10*. Brighton: IDS.

Leader, N. & Colenso, P. (2005). 'Aid Instruments in Fragile States'. *PRDE Working Paper 5*. London: DFID.

Lee, K., Sridhar, D. & Patel, M. (2009). 'Bridging the divide: global governance of trade and health'. *The Lancet* 373: 416–22.

Lensink, R. & White, H. (1999). 'Is There an Aid Laffer Curve?'. *CREDIT Working Paper 99/6*. Nottingham: University of Nottingham, Centre for Research in Economic Development and International Trade.

Lensink, R. & White, H. (2001). 'Are there Negative Returns to Aid?'. *Journal of Development Studies* 37: 42–65.

Levin, V. & Dollar, D. (2005). 'The Forgotten States: Aid Volumes and Volatility in Difficult Partnerships Countries (1992–2002)'. *Paper for DAC Learning and Advisory Process on Difficult Partnerships*. Washington, DC: World Bank.

Liese, B., Rosenburg, M. & Schratz, A. (2010). 'Programmes, Partnerships, and Governance for Elimination and Control of Neglected Tropical Diseases'. *Lancet* 375: 67–76.

Llavador, H. G. & Roemer, J. E. (2001). 'An Equal-opportunity Approach to the Allocation of International Aid'. *Journal of Development Economics* 64: 147–71.

Lob-Levyt, J. & Affolder, R. (2006). 'Innovative Financing for Human Development'. *Lancet* 367: 885–887.

Lockhart, C. (2005). 'From Aid Effectiveness to Development Effectiveness: Strategy and Policy Coherence in Fragile States'. *Background paper for the Senior Level Forum on Development Effectiveness in Fragile States*. London: Overseas Development Institute.

Loxley, J. & Sackey, H. (2008). 'Aid Effectiveness in Africa'. *African Development Review* 20(2): 163–99.

Luckham, R. with Gyimah-Boadi, E., Ahadzie, W. & Boateng, N. (2005). 'The Middle Classes and their Role in National Development'. *Policy Brief 3*. CDD/ODI.

Macdonald, R. & Hoddinott, J. (2004). 'Determinants of Canadian Bilateral Aid Allocations: Humanitarian, Commercial or Political?'. *Canadian Journal of Economics* 37(2): 294–312.

Manning, R. (2006). 'Will "Emerging Donors" Change the Face of International Co-operation?'. *Development Policy Review* 24(4): 371–85.

Mansuri, G. (2006). 'Migration, School Attainment and Child Labor: Evidence from Rural Pakistan'. *Policy Research Working Paper 3945*. Washintgon, DC: World Bank.

Markandya, A., Ponczek, V. & Yi, S. (2010). 'What Are the Links between Aid Volatility and Growth?'. *Policy Research Working Paper 5201*. Washington, DC: World Bank.

Mavrotas, G. (2005). 'Aid Heterogeneity: Looking at Aid Effectiveness from a Different Angle'. *Journal of International Development* 17: 1019–36.

Mawdsley, E. (2010). 'Non-DAC Donors and the Changing Landscape of Foreign Aid: The (In)Significance of India's Development Cooperation with Kenya'. *Journal of Eastern African Studies* 4(2): 361–79.

Mawdsley, E. (2012). 'The Changing Geographies of Foreign Aid and Development Cooperation: Contributions from Gift Theory'. *Transactions of the Institute of British Geographers* 37(2): 256-72.

Mayer, T. (2006). 'Policy Coherence for Development: A Background Paper on Foreign Direct Investment'. *Working Paper 253*. Paris: OECD Development Centre.

McCormick, D. (2008). 'China and India as Africa's New Donors: The Impact of Aid on Development'. *Review of African Political Economy* 35(115): 73–92.

McCoy, D. (2009). 'The High Level Taskforce on Innovative International Financing for Health Systems'. *Health Policy and Planning* 24: 321–23.

McGee, R., Levene, J. & Hughes, A. (2002). 'Assessing Participation in Poverty Reduction Strategy Papers: a desk-based synthesis of experience in Sub-Saharan Africa'. *IDS Research Report 52*. Brighton: Institute of Development Studies.

McGillivray, M. (1989). 'The Allocation of Aid among Developing Countries: A Multi-Donor Analysis Using a Per Capita Aid Index'. *World Development* 17(4): 561–68.

McGillivray, M. (2003). 'Aid Effectiveness and Selectivity: Integrating Multiple Objectives into Aid Allocations'. *Discussion Paper 2003/71*. Helsinki: UNU-WIDER.

McGillivray, M. (2006). 'Aid Allocation and Fragile States'. *Discussion Paper 2006/01*. Helsinki: UNU-WIDER.

McGillivray, M. & Feeny, S. (2008). 'Aid and Growth in Fragile States'. *UNU-WIDER Research Paper 2008/03*. Helsinki: UNU-WIDER.

McGillivray, M. & Feeny, S. (2009). 'Aid Allocation to Fragile States: Absorptive Capacity Constraints'. *Journal of International Development* 21(5): 618–32.

McGillivray, M. & Morrissey, O. (2000). 'Aid fungibility in *Assessing Aid*: red herring or true concern?'. *Journal of International Development* 12(3): 413–28.

McGillivray, M., Feeny, S., Hermes, N. & Lensink, R. (2006). 'Controversies of the Development Impact of Aid: It Works; it doesn't; it can, but that depends...'. *Journal of International Development* 18(7): 1031–50.

Michaelowa, A. & Michaelowa, K. (2005). 'Climate or development: Is ODA diverted from its original purpose?'. *HWWI Research Paper 2*. Hamburg: HWWI.

Milstien, J. B., Kamara, L., Lydon, P., Mitchell, V. & Landry, S. (2008). 'The GAVI Financing Task Force: One Model of partner collaboration'. *Vaccine* 26: 6699–705.

Molenaers, N. & Renard, R. (2002). 'Strengthening Civil Society from the Outside? Donor-driven Consultation and Participation Processes in Poverty Reduction Strategies (PRSP): the Bolivian Case'. Prepared for the 2002 Annual Meeting of the American Political Science Association, August 29-September 1.

Moody's (2011). Sovereigns ratings. [Registration required].

Moore, M. (2001). *Types of Political Systems: A Practical Framework for DFID Staff*. London: DFID.

Moore, M. (2004). 'Revenues, State Formation, and the Quality of Governance in Developing Countries'. *International Political Science Review* 25(3): 297–319.

Morrissey, O. (2001). 'Does aid increase growth?'. *Progress in Development Studies* 1(1): 37–50.

Mosley, P. & Suleiman, A. (2007). 'Aid, Agriculture and Poverty in Developing Countries'. *Review of Development Economics* 11(1): 139–58.

Mosley, P., Hudson, J. & Verschoor, A. (2004). 'Aid, Poverty Reduction and the "New Conditionality"'. *The Economic Journal* 114: 217–43.

Moss, T. & Leo, B. (2011). 'IDA at 65: Heading Toward Retirement or a Fragile Lease on Life?'. *Working Paper 246.* Washington, DC: Center for Global Development.

Moss, T., Pettersson, G. & van de Walle, N. (2006). 'An Aid-Institutions Paradox? A Review Essay on Aid Dependency and State Building in Sub-Saharan Africa'. *Working Paper 74.* Washington, DC: Center for Global Development

Neumayer, E. (2003). *The Pattern of Aid Giving—The Impact of Good Governance on Development Finance.* London: Routledge.

NORAD (2009). 'The Global Health Landscape and Innovative International Financing for Health Systems: trends and issues'. Draft, prepared by NORAD-AHHA.

North, D. C. (1995). 'The New Institutional Economics and Third World Development'. In Harriss, J., Hunter, J. & Lewis, C. M. (eds) *The New Institutional Economics and Third World Development*, pp. 17–26. London: Routledge.

Nunnenkamp, P. & Thiele, R. (2006). 'Targeting Aid to the Needy and Deserving: Nothing But Promises?'. *The World Economy* 29(9): 1177–201.

ODI (2004). 'Inequality in Middle Income Countries'. *Briefing Paper.* London: ODI.

OECD (2002). 'Action for a Shared Development Agenda'. *Ministerial Statement.* Paris: OECD.

OECD (2006). *International Development Statistics On-Line.* Paris: OECD.

OECD (2007). *The Principles for Good International Engagement in Fragile States and Situations.* Paris: OECD.

OECD (2008). *Is it ODA? Factsheet – November 2008.* Paris: OECD.

OECD (2010). *Resource flows to Fragile and Conflict Affected States.* Paris: OECD.

Ohno, I. & Niiya, Y. (2004). *Good Donorship and the Choice of Aid Modalities: Matching Aid with Country Needs and Ownership.* Tokyo: GRIPS Development Forum.

Ostrom, E., Gibson, C., Shivakumar, S. & Andersson, K. (2001). 'Aid, Incentives and Sustainability: An Institutional Analysis of Development Cooperation'. *Mimeo*. Bloomington: Workshop in Political theory and Policy Analysis, Indiana University.

Ottaway, M. (2003). 'Rebuilding State Institutions in Collapsed States'. In Milliken, J. (ed.) *State Failure, Collapse & Reconstruction*, pp. 245–266. Oxford: Blackwell.

Ouattara, B. (2006). 'Foreign Aid and Government Fiscal Behaviour in Developing Countries: Panel Data Evidence'. *Economic Modelling* 23(3): 506–14.

Ouattara, B. (2007). 'Foreign Aid, Public Savings Displacement and Aid Dependency in Cote d'Ivoire: An Aid Disaggregation Approach'. *Oxford Development Studies* 35(1): 33–46.

Oxfam (2011). 'Whose Aid is it Anyway? Politicizing Aid in Conflicts and Crises'. *Oxfam Briefing Paper*. Oxford: Oxfam.

Papanek, G. F. (1973). 'Aid, Foreign Private Investment, Savings, and Growth in Less Developed Countries'. *Journal of Political Economy* 81(1): 120–30.

Quartey, P. (2005). 'Innovative Ways of Making Aid Effective in Ghana: Tied Versus Direct Budgetary Support'. *Journal of International Development* 17: 1077–92.

Quazi, R. M. (2005). 'Effects of Foreign Aid on GDP Growth and Fiscal Behavior: An Econometric Case Study of Bangladesh'. *Journal of Developing Areas* 38(2): 95–117.

Paris, R. (2004). *At War's End: Building Peace after Civil Conflict*. Cambridge: Cambridge University

Paris, R. & Sisk, T. D. (2007). 'Managing Contradictions: The Inherent Dilemmas of Postwar Statebuilding'. *Research Partnership on Postwar Statebuilding*. New York, NY: International Peace Academy.

Patrick, S. & Brown, K. (2006). 'Fragile States and US Foreign Assistance: Show Me the Money'. *Working Paper 96*. Washington, DC: Center for Global Development.

Paulo, S. & Reisen, H. (2010). 'Eastern Donors and Western Soft Law: Towards a DAC Donor Peer Review of China and India?'. *Development Policy Review* 28(5): 535–52.

Pessoa, A. (2008). 'Public-Private Partnerships in Developing Countries: Are Infrastructures Responding to the New ODA Strategy?'. *Journal of International Development* 20: 311–25.

Picciotto, R. (2005). 'The Evaluation of Policy Coherence for Development'. *Evaluation* 11(3): 311–30.
Pronk, J. P. (2001). 'Aid as a Catalyst'. *Development and Change* 32: 611–29.
Radelet, S. (2006). 'A Primer on Foreign Aid'. *Working Paper 92*. Washington, DC: Center for Global Development.
Rajan, R. G. & Subramanian, A. (2005). 'Aid and Growth: What Does the Cross-Country Evidence Really Show?'. *Working Paper 05/127*. Washington, DC: IMF.
Ram, R. (2004). 'Recipient Country's "Policies" and the Effect of Foreign Aid on Economic Growth in Developing Countries: Additional Evidence'. *Journal of International Development* 16: 201–11.
Ramalingam, B. & Jones, H. with Reba, T. & Young, J. (2008). 'Exploring the Science of Complexity: Ideas and Implications for Development and Humanitarian Efforts'. *Working Paper 285*. London: Overseas Development Institute.
Ratha, D., Mohapatra, S. & Plaza, S. (2008). 'Beyond Aid: New Source and Innovative Mechanisms for Financing Development in Sub-Saharan Africa'. *Policy Research Working Paper 4609*. Washington, DC: World Bank.
Ratha, D., Mohapatra, S. & Scheja, E. (2011). 'Impact of Migration on Economic and Social Development: A Review of Evidence and Emerging Issues'. *Policy Research Working Paper 5558*. Washington, DC: World Bank.
Ratha, D., Mohapatra, S. & Silwal, A. (2010). 'Outlook for Remittance Flows 2010–11'. *Migration and Development Brief 12*. Washington, DC: World Bank.
Ravallion, M. (2009). 'Do Poorer Countries have less Capacity for Redistribution?'. *Policy Research Working Paper 5046*. Washington, DC: World Bank.
Ravallion, M. (2009). 'The Developing World's Bulging (but Vulnerable) "Middle Class"'. *Policy Research Working Paper 4816*. Washington, DC: World Bank.
Rawlings, L. B. (2004). 'A New Approach to Social Assistance: Latin America's Experience with Conditional Cash Transfer Programs'. *Social Protection Discussion Paper Series 0416*. Washington, DC: World Bank.
Reisen, H. (2003). 'New Sources of Development Finance: An Annotated Conference Report'. Paris: OECD.

Riddell, R. C. (1986). 'The Ethics of Foreign Aid'. *Development Policy Review*, 4(1): 24–43.

Riddell, R. C. (2007). *Does Foreign Aid Really Work?*. Oxford: Oxford University.

Roberts, D. (2008). 'Hybrid Polities and Indigenous Pluralities: Advanced Lessons in Statebuilding from Cambodia'. *Journal of Intervention and Statebuilding* 2(1): 63–86.

Robinson, M. (1995). 'Strengthening Civil Society in Africa: The Role of Foreign Political Aid'. *IDS Bulletin* 26(2): 70–80.

Robinson, M. & Friedman, S. (2007). 'Civil Society, Democratization, and Foreign Aid: Civic Engagement and Public Policy in South Africa and Uganda'. *Democratization* 14(4): 643–68.

Rogerson, A. (2011). 'What If Development Aid Were Truly "Catalytic"?'. *Background Note*. London: Overseas Development Institute.

Roodman, D. (2004). 'The Anarchy of Numbers: Aid, Development and Cross-Country Empirics'. *Working Paper 32*. Washington, DC: CGD.

Roodman, D. (2007). 'The Anarchy of Numbers: Aid, Development, and Cross-Country Empirics'. *World Bank Economic Review* 21(2): 255–277.

Roodman, D. (2010). *The Commitment to Development Index: 2010 Edition*. Washington, DC: CGD.

Rosenstein-Rodan, P. N. (1961). 'International Aid for Underdeveloped Countries'. *Review of Economics and Statistics* 43: 107–38.

Rostoski, K. (2006) 'Development Cooperation between Germany and China: Does China still need Development Aid?'. *Asia-Europe Journal* 4: 539–44.

Ruhashyankiko, J. (2005). 'Why do Some Countries manage to extract Growth from Foreign Aid?'. *Working Paper 05/53*. Washington, DC: IMF.

Sachs, J. D. (2005a). 'The Development Challenge'. *Foreign Affairs* 84: 78–90.

Sachs, J. D. (2005b). *The End of Poverty: Economic Possibilities For Our Time*. New York, NY: Penguin.

Samoff, J. & Stromquist, N. P. (2001). 'Managing Knowledge and Storing Wisdom? New Forms of Foreign Aid?'. *Development and Change* 32(4): 631–56.

Sandor, E. (2008). 'Lessons for Development Finance from Innovative Financing in Health'. Informal Experts' Workshop, OECD Global Forum on Development, 7 October.

Santiso, C. (2001). 'International Co-operation for Democracy and Good Governance: Moving Towards a Second Generation?'. *European Journal of Development Research* 13(1): 154–80.

Sayanak, T. & Lahiri, S. (2009). 'Foreign Aid as Prize: Incentives for a Pro-Poor Policy'. *Review of Development Economics* 13(3): 403–15.

Senauer, B. & Goetz, L. (2003). 'The Growing Middle Class in Developing Countries and the Market for High-Value Food Products'. Prepared for the Workshop on Global Markets for High-Value Food, Washington, DC, 14 February.

Senge, P. M. (1990). *The Fifth Discipline: The Art and Practice of the Learning* Organisation. New York, NY: Doubleday Currency.

Severino, J-M. & Ray, O. (2009). 'The End of ODA: Death and Rebirth of a Global Public Policy'. *Working Paper 167.* Washington, DC: Center for Global Development.

Severino, J-M. & Ray, O. (2010). 'The End of ODA (II): The Birth of Hypercollective Action'. *Working Paper 218.* Washington, DC: Center for Global Development.

Smith, R. D. & MacKellar, L. (2007). 'Global Public Goods and the Global Health Agenda: Problems, Priorities and Potential'. *Globalization and Health* 3: 9.

Sollis, P. (1994). 'The Relief-Development Continuum'. *Journal of International Affairs* 47(2): 451–71.

Standard and Poor's (2011). Sovereigns ratings list. http://www.standardandpoors.com/ratings/sovereigns/ratings-list/en/us/?sectorName=Governments&subSectorCode=39&start=0&range=50. Accessed 1 April 2011.

Stewart, F. & Wang, M. (2003). 'Do PRSPs Empower Poor Countries and Disempower the World Bank, or is it the other Way Round?'. *Working Paper 108.* Oxford: Oxford University.

Stansfield, S. K., Harper, M., Lamb, G. & Lob-Levyt, J. (2002). 'Innovative Financing of International Public Goods for Health'. *CMH Working Paper Series, No. WG2: 22.* Commission on Macroeconomics and Health, WHO

Sumner, A. (2010). 'Global Poverty and the New Bottom Billion'. *IDS Working Paper 349.* Brighton: IDS.

Sumner, A. (2012a) Where do the Poor Live? *World Development* 40(5), 865–87.

Sumner, A. (2012b). Where do the World's Poor Live? A New Update *IDS Working Paper*. Brighton: IDS.

Sumner, A. (2012c). From Deprivation to Distribution: Is Global Poverty Becoming A Matter of National Inequality? *IDS Working Paper*. Brighton: IDS.

Sumner, A. (2012d, forthcoming) 'Poverty, Vulnerability and Class: The Expanding Non-Polar Groups and Development', *Public Administration and Development*.

Sumner, A., & Tiwari, M. (2009). *After 2015: International Development Policy at a Crossroads*. Basingstoke: Palgrave Macmillan.

Sumner, A. & Tribe, M. (2011) The Case for Aid in Fiscally Constrained Times. *Journal of International Development*. 23(6), 782–801.

Sumner, A., Mitchell., T and Tanner, T. (2010). Future-proofing the MDGs: What are the critical uncertainties for 2010–2015 and beyond? Annex to: What are the implications of the global crisis and its aftermath for developing countries, 2010–2020? *IPC-IG Working Paper Number 68*. Brasilia. IPC-IG:

Suhrke, A. & Buckmaster, J. (2006). 'Aid, Growth and Peace: A Comparative Analysis'. *Conflict, Security and Development* 6(3): 337–63.

Suhrke, A., Villanger, E. & Woodward, S. L. (2005). 'Economic Aid to Post-Conflict Countries: A Methodological Critique of Collier and Hoeffler'. *CMI Working Paper 2005: 4*. Bergen: Chr. Michelsen Institute.

Svensson, J. (1999). 'Aid, Growth and Democracy'. *Economics and Politics* 11(3): 275–97.

Svensson, J. (2000). 'Why Conditional Aid does not Work and What Can Be Done about It?'. *Journal of Development Economics* 70: 381–402.

Taskforce on Innovative International Financing for Health Systems (2009). 'Raising and Channeling Funds'. *Working Group 2 Report*. Geneva / Washington, DC: International Health Partnership.

Task Team on South-South Cooperation (2011). 'Call for Case Stories: Knowledge exchange as an effective tool for development'. http://www.southsouth.org/pdf/call_for_case_stories_2011.pdf Accessed 1 April 2011.

te Velde, D. W., Morrissey, O. & Hewitt, A. (2002). 'Allocating Aid to International Public Goods'. In Ferroni, M. & Mody, A. (eds) *International Public Goods: Incentives, Measurement, and Financing*. Washington, DC: World Bank.

Van Tuijl, P. (2000). 'Entering the Global Dealing Room: Reflections on a Rights-based Framework for NGOs in International Development'. *Third World Quarterly* 21(4): 617–26.

Verschoor, A. & Kalwij, A. (2006). 'Aid, Social Policies and Pro-Poor Growth'. *Journal of International Development* 18: 519–32.

Vidal, C. & Pillay, R. (2004). 'Official Development Assistance as Direct Budget Support: An Issues Paper for UNDP'. Prepared for BRSP/UNDP.

Warrener, D. (2004). 'The Drivers of Change Approach'. *Synthesis Paper 3*. London: Overseas Development Institute.

Webster, N. & Engberg-Pedersen, L. (eds) (2002). *In the Name of the Poor: Contesting Political Space for Poverty Reduction*. London: Zed.

Weiss, J. (2008). 'The Aid Paradigm for Poverty Reduction: Does it Make Sense?'. *Development Policy Review* 26(4): 407–26.

Wheary, J. (2009). 'The Global Middle Class is Here: Now What?'. *World Policy Journal* Winter 2009/10: 75–83.

White, H. (2001). 'Will the New Aid Agenda Help Promote Poverty Reduction?'. *Journal of International Development* 13: 1057–70.

Whitfield, L. & Fraser, A. (2009). 'Negotiating Aid'. In Whitfield, L. (ed.) *The Politics of Aid: African Strategies for Dealing with Donors*. Oxford: Oxford University.

Wood, A. (2008). 'Looking Ahead Optimally in Allocating Aid'. *World Development* 36(7): 1135–51.

Wood, B., Kabell, D., Muwanga, N. & Sagasti, F. (2008). *Synthesis Report on the First Phase of the Evaluation of the Implementation of the Paris Declaration*. Copenhagen: Danish Ministry of Foreign Affairs.

World Bank (1998). *Assessing Aid: What Works, What Doesn't and Why*. Washington, DC: World Bank.

Xenogiani, T. (2006). 'Migration Policy and Its Interactions with Aid, Trade and Foreign Direct Investment Policies: A Background Paper'. *Working Paper 249*. Paris: OECD.

Younas, J. (2008). 'Motivation for Bilateral Aid Allocation: Altruism or Trade Benefits'. *European Journal of Political Economy* 24(3): 661–74.

Index

aid:
  allocations, 14, 21–27, 35, 43
  effectiveness, 4–5, 28–38, 48, 63–73
  instruments, 2, 6, 10–20, 29, 35, 36, 47, 48, 50, 58, 59
  objectives, 4, 6, 10–14, 17, 21–27, 33, 40–45, 46–59

Brazil, 11, 12, 53
budget support, 12–16, 30, 47
business/private sector, 5, 15–20, 57

cash transfer, 17, 48, 59
charity, 51
China, 2, 11, 12, 13, 14, 43, 56, 59
climate/climate change, 6, 13, 19, 22, 23, 44, 55, 65, 67
climate financing, 18, 56, 58
Common Agricultural Policy (CAP), 50
conflict, 5, 23, 36–37, 49, 65, 70, 73

democracy, 22, 23, 31, 35, 48, 52, 64, 69, 70
donor, 2–6, 11–19, 22–27, 30–31, 35–37, 43–59, 62, 72
Dutch disease, 32, 36, 66

economic growth, 5, 14, 22–27, 31–34, 37, 49, 63–73
European Union, 50

fragile and conflict-affected state (FCAS)/fragile state, 10, 11, 14, 16, 26, 36–37, 47–48, 62, 67

GAVI, 17, 57
GDP/per capita GDP, 3, 13, 30, 32, 41–44, 68, 71
Ghana, 49
global public goods, 6, 17, 18, 36, 49, 54–58, 61–62

income/per capita income, 2, 22–26, 37–38, 42, 44, 64, 65, 67, 71, 73
India, 5, 7, 11, 12, 13, 43, 49, 69
Indonesia, 5, 7, 49, 56
inequality, 2, 6, 26, 41, 42, 71
innovative finance/financing, 2, 17–19, 36, 56, 57
institutions, 33–38, 47–48, 51–55, 63, 65, 70
investment, 13–14, 23, 30–35, 43, 49, 50–53, 56, 66, 68, 69, 70, 71

lower middle-income country (LMIC), 3, 42, 44
low-income country (LIC), 2–7, 10–13, 26–27, 32, 36–38, 42–49, 58–59, 62, 67, 72

middle-income country (MIC), 2–7, 10–14, 25–26, 36–38, 42–59, 62, 67, 70
migration, 3, 18–20, 46, 50–51, 62
Millennium Development Goals (MDGs), 2, 4, 14, 17, 22, 26, 48

Nigeria, 5, 49

official development assistance (ODA), 2–7, 12–19, 24, 26, 43–49, 58–59, 61–62
Organisation for Economic Cooperation and Development (OECD), 11–15, 20, 44, 49–50

Pakistan, 5, 7, 49, 69
Paris Declaration, 16–17, 30
peace-building/state-building, 48, 59
per capita GDP. *See* GDP/per capita GDP
per capita income. *See* income/per capita income
philanthropy/philanthropists, 2
policy coherence, 17, 19–20, 45–46, 49–51, 61–62
pollution, 54
poverty, 2–7, 14, 25–26, 29, 31, 35, 37, 40–45, 48–54, 60–65, 71, 73

poverty reduction, 2–4, 10, 19–33, 37, 42–43, 47, 49, 56, 63, 71–72
Poverty Reduction Strategy Paper (PRSP), 16, 30
private sector. *See* business/private sector

recipient, 4, 5, 10–19, 22–27, 30–36, 50, 54, 57, 63, 65, 67–68, 70–71, 73
regional public goods, 17, 56
research, 10, 33–35, 46–47, 55–56, 58, 62, 66

social protection, 13, 17, 48
South Africa, 53, 72
state-building. *See* peace-building/state-building

tariffs, 50–51
tax, 2, 5, 18, 30, 43–44, 51, 57–58, 61, 69
trade, 4–6, 14, 19–20, 22–23, 34, 45–50, 56, 62, 64, 65, 67

Uganda, 30, 53, 72
United Kingdom, 53
United States, 22, 25, 26
upper middle-income country (UMIC), 3, 42, 44

World Bank, 2, 10, 11, 59, 64, 68, 70

CPSIA information can be obtained at www.ICGtesting.com
Printed in the USA
LVOW130908110113

315340LV00003B/114/P